MW00712856

A Barna Report Produced
in Partnership with Boone
Center for the Family

RESTORING RELATIONSHIPS

HOW CHURCHES CAN HELP PEOPLE HEAL
& DEVELOP HEALTHY CONNECTIONS

Copyright © 2020 by Barna Group. All rights reserved.

ISBN: 978-1-945269-54-7

All information contained in this document is copyrighted by Barna Group and shall remain the property of Barna Group. U.S. and international copyright laws protect the contents of this document in their entirety. Any reproduction, modification, distribution, transmission, publication, translation, display, hosting or sale of all or any portion of the contents of this document is strictly prohibited without written permission of an authorized representative of Barna Group.

The information contained in this report is true and accurate to the best knowledge of the copyright holder. It is provided without warranty of any kind: express, implied or otherwise. In no event shall Barna Group or its respective officers or employees be liable for any special, incidental, indirect or consequential damages of any kind, or any damages whatsoever resulting from the use of this information, whether or not users have been advised of the possibility of damage, or on any theory of liability, arising out of or in connection with the use of this information.

Funding for this research was made possible by the generous support of the Boone Center for the Family. Barna Group was solely responsible for data collection, analysis and writing of the report.

CONTENTS

5
PREFACE
by Sharon Hargrave, LMFT

9
INTRODUCTION

15
1. WHAT IS THE STATE OF RELATIONAL HEALTH TODAY?
"The Ambiguous Loss of Unwanted Singleness," by Kelly Maxwell Haer, PhD
"A Church Family for Young Adults (& Everyone Else)," a Q&A with Katelyn Beaty

36
SPECIAL SECTION: VISUALIZING THE ISSUES
Marital Issues
Unwanted Singleness
Parenting Issues
Sexual Intimacy
Addiction
Anxiety / Depression
Pornography
Loneliness

47
2. HOW ARE RELATIONSHIPS UNDER PRESSURE?
"Helping Young People into Healthy Relationships," a Q&A with Michael Cox
"Anxiety, Depression & Avoiding Pastoral Burnout," a Q&A with Rhett Smith
"Healing Addiction in the Church," a Q&A with Tal Prince

75
3. WHERE DO PEOPLE TURN FOR SUPPORT
& HOW CAN CHURCHES HELP?
"The Gospel Significance of Emotional Health," a Q&A with Mike Boland
"Washing the Wounds of Racial Trauma," a Q&A with Chris Williamson
"Healthy Ways to Help the Opposite Sex," a Q&A with Thema Bryant-Davis & Cameron Lee

97
CONCLUSION: PARTNERS IN RESTORATION

101
APPENDIX
A. Notes
B. Methodology

105
ACKNOWLEDGMENTS

106
ABOUT THE PROJECT PARTNERS

PREFACE

By Sharon Hargrave, LMFT

In a world where trauma, emotional pain and relational disconnection are pervasive, healing can seem unattainable. However, I am convinced that even in the most poignant suffering, there is a way to transformative healing. I know because I have experienced it firsthand.

When I was three, my father died by suicide. My oldest brother, Bruce, died suddenly of acute leukemia when I was four. My second-oldest brother, David, and his date were murdered when I was 13. Bipolar disorder runs rampant in my family, and addiction is present in every generation. Yet in my adult years, I have lived a somewhat normal life: happily married for 40 years with two adult children who love to come home. Since we know trauma is a disrupter in stable, loving relationships, what makes my story different?

For me, it was the combination of church and therapy. When I was young, my home church held my family and me close. We had men who fathered us and families who gathered around us. Organizations like Navigators and Young Life taught me deep, biblical truths and how to enjoy a life following Christ. A Christian camp near my hometown made every summer a three-month reprieve when "family" surrounded me and gave me identity.

When I was older, my studies to become a marriage and family therapist taught me about relational attachment, the importance of defining myself outside of my trauma and why it was difficult for me to commit to marriage and having children. In the early years, I would have told you the problems in my marriage were because of my husband. I didn't understand that the childhood trauma I had experienced was creeping into my adult life.

The therapy world has told us to get rid of toxic people in our lives; the Church, on the other hand, has told us to forgive everyone. Both perspectives offer some truth.

In my journey as a Christian and as a therapist, I have watched these two perspectives seem to drift apart. The therapy world has told us to have strong boundaries and to get rid of toxic people in our lives—contributing, I think, to the highest rates of anxiety, depression and loneliness ever recorded. The Church, on the other hand, has told us to forgive everyone, leaving people in destructive relationships that crush identity. Both perspectives offer some truth. We *do* need to have the strength to get away from extremely damaging relationships. However, we must also realize that everyone in our lives will make mistakes—as will we—and cutting everyone out of our lives doesn't solve the problem.

Do Christians understand that it is okay to make mistakes, to have family problems, to struggle with anxiety or fall into an addiction? What if these trials enter my family system? Does it make me less of a Christian for me or my family to struggle?

As executive director of the Boone Center for the Family at Pepperdine University, and as a person committed to helping Christian leaders live well, I think a lot about what Christians and mental health-care providers can do to help people connect and build strong ties. In commissioning this study with Barna, our team wanted to know how churches are doing both in helping people deepen relationships and in supporting those who are struggling with relationships and mental health concerns. We wanted to know whether practicing Christians as well as non-Christians see the Church as a place to receive hope and healing. We wondered if pastors feel prepared to help relationships heal and to give guidance to those dealing with mental health problems. How can our center help leaders deal with their own issues related to marriage, parenting, singleness and healthy intimacy, while also coaching them to help individuals and families through the pain of issues like pornography, addiction, anxiety and depression? How can churches and mental healthcare providers work together?

One of the many significant findings in this study indicates that people who address their relationship concerns and mental health struggles *at church* experience greater spiritual growth. Bearing one another's burdens, it seems, does lighten the load (see Galatians 6). Whether we are church leaders or mental healthcare providers, our common goal should be to help people lay aside destructive, damaging ways of coping (in Christian terms, the "old self") and live into connecting, constructive, life-giving relationships ("new-self" living).

> People who address their relationship concerns at church experience greater spiritual growth. Bearing one another's burdens, it seems, does lighten the load.

My prayer is that this research shows us how to bring hope and healing to those who need help. Individuals and families are struggling. But there is help to be found! I know, because church and therapy helped me cope with pain, learn to experience joy and live in the family and community God used to make me whole.

SHARON HARGRAVE is executive director for the Boone Center for the Family at Pepperdine University and Founder of RelateStrong. She is also an affiliate faculty member at Fuller Theological Seminary and a licensed marriage and family therapist in California and Texas. Sharon and her husband, Terry, speak nationally and internationally on issues related to couples in ministry, marriage, intergenerational relationships, parenting and the Restoration Therapy model. She is coauthor with her husband of *5 Days to a New Self*.

STUDY OVERVIEW

PHASE 1. QUALITATIVE INTERVIEWS

Researchers sat down with counselors, pastors and other experts with a handful of open-ended questions, which were designed to get them talking about what they're seeing in their ministries and counseling practices when it comes to people's relationships. The findings from this phase helped researchers design hypotheses to test using quantitative surveys.

PHASE 2. SURVEY DESIGN & FIELDING

Based on qualitative findings, researchers created two surveys that were then administered online to more than 2,000 U.S. adults and 600 U.S. pastors and priests.

PHASE 3. ANALYSIS

Data analysts combed through the data to test and verify survey results, then ran statistical analyses to uncover significance. Deeper analysis was completed over several months.

INTRODUCTION

Relationships are under pressure. This pressure is new, and it's unique in human history. Squeezed between massive changes in communication technologies, diminishing religious influence, hyperindividualized morals and sexual ethics and extreme cultural and political polarization, the strain on our everyday relationships is mounting—and it's not always clear to people where they can turn for help. For that matter, it's not always clear to those in the thick of relational crisis—whether because of trauma, isolation, mental illness or just the everyday challenges of life—that they are not alone. (Loneliness is at epidemic levels, and experiencing it magnifies otherwise manageable challenges.)

Relational crises are no respecter of persons—that is, they happen to just about everybody at one time or another: women and men, younger and older, single and married, Christian and non-Christian. Any relationship can face problems (if we're not in a relationship of any kind, that's an issue all its own!) and anyone can experience challenges to their mental, emotional or relational health. It's just a fact of life.

On the whole, the Church's record on helping people through crisis is strong. Historically, pastors and other church leaders have been uniquely positioned to walk alongside people through their hardest seasons in life: death of a loved one, job loss, illness, divorce, unwanted singleness, childlessness, abuse and so much more. With the rise of human psychology as a scientific discipline, however, people have options beyond their local church or parish. Church leaders, for their part, have not always been enthusiastic supporters of mental health science . . . especially when therapeutic professionals and approaches deny a spiritual dimension to human well-being.

Relational crises happen to just about everybody at one time or another: women and men, younger and older, single and married, Christian and non-Christian

Between the upsurge in non-pastoral helping professions and the rapid secularization of younger generations, what's a pastor to do? Just relinquish their traditional role as relational counselor and spiritual coach?

The answer is a resounding no.

Restoring Relationships unpacks the implications of data gathered from more than 2,300 U.S. adults and 650 U.S. pastors and priests—and the overwhelming takeaway is that churches have a supremely important role to play in helping people grow through their relational challenges. (For a complete methodology of the study, see page 103.)

GOOD FAITH

Barna's president, David Kinnaman, often says that people want to know that Christianity is both true and good. This is particularly true for Millennials and Gen Z, age cohorts that collectively tend toward a holistic view of human flourishing that includes mental and emotional health. At the same time, many of them (and people in older generations, too) report dealing with anxiety, depression, addiction, marital problems and other issues that negatively impact their relationships (take an up-close look at the issues people say they are dealing with in the special data visualization section on pages 36–45).

What an incredible, wide-open door for the Church! Christ makes all things new, transforming us and our relationships. People's longing for true and lasting transformation from the inside out is an opportunity for the Church to bring good news where people want to hear it: in the places where they're hurting and most in need of healing.

Mental health professionals have an important role to play, too. Whether it's helping pastors better understand the brain science of addiction, bringing clinically sound tools to a marriage that's in trouble or coaching parents through the heartbreak of a child's mental illness, trained and licensed counselors are specialists in the hardest parts of being human. Imagine the powerful partnership that pastors and Christ-centered mental health pros can create to help people restore their relationships through the power of God's Spirit.

> People's longing for transformation is an opportunity to bring good news where people want to hear it: where they're hurting and most in need of healing

In *Restoring Relationships,* you'll find not only brand-new data on the state of relationships in America today, but also profound insights from both pastors and professional counselors on how churches can help people heal. In some ways, this report is a reference guide for what's going on in your congregation—and how people wish you and your church could help.

Let's dive in.

KEY FINDINGS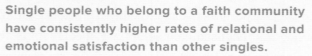

Relational well-being and satisfaction are high across the board, but married people and parents tend to be more content overall than singles and people without children. Practicing Christians (both married and single) are also more likely than non-Christians to say they are satisfied.

Single people who belong to a faith community have consistently higher rates of relational and emotional satisfaction than other singles.

More than half of all U.S. adults (58%) and practicing Christians (54%) say they have at least one relational or emotional / mental health issue that impacts their most important relationships.

Anxiety and depression are the most commonly experienced challenges to relational satisfaction, with more than one-third of all adults and practicing Christians saying one or the other (or both) make an impact on their close relationships.

Relational, emotional and mental health problems often aggravate and intensify each other. For example, a person who says that pornography impacts her most important relationships is also more likely than average to say she's dealing with anxiety, loneliness and problems with sexual intimacy.

People who seek out spiritual help for their relational and emotional issues are more likely than others to report satisfaction with their life and relationships.

Practicing Christians are generally confident that their church leaders can help them with their relational struggles—but many agree there is room for improvement.

— 1 —

WHAT IS THE STATE OF RELATIONAL HEALTH TODAY?

Relationships exist within a specific culture—and that means cultural change can profoundly shape our relationships. Whether they're cultural trends related to cohabitation, delayed marriage, delayed parenting, working parents, telecommuting or social media, or changes in attitudes toward marriage, singleness, children, aging, friendships and community—all of these impact the formation and development of family and friendship. Even national policies—such as tax credits for childcare and education, or China's former longstanding one-child policy—can shape household composition and relational dynamics.

It has been two decades since sociologist Robert Putnam released *Bowling Alone,* which documented rising community disengagement among Americans. Despite Putnam's warnings, the problem of loneliness seems to have grown.[1] A 2018 Cigna study of more than 20,000 U.S. adults ages 18 years and older revealed that "nearly half of Americans report sometimes or always feeling alone (46)," and that 43 percent of Americans "sometimes or always feel that their relationships are not meaningful."[2] The youngest group of respondents, ages 18 to 22, are the loneliest age cohort, pointing to an increasing trend of loneliness in younger generations. Likewise, Barna's 2019 study of 18–35-year-olds around the world, *The Connected Generation,* found that that one-quarter of Millennials (23%) reports they often feel lonely and isolated.[3] At the same time, just one in three often feels that "someone believes in me" (32%).

Barna's 2019 study of 18–35-year-olds around the world found that one-quarter of Millennials reports they often feel lonely and isolated; only one in three often feel that someone believes in them

One factor that may exacerbate the loneliness epidemic is the social expectation to marry and start a family, which has a long history reaching back to ancient cultures. Tim Keller, founding pastor of Redeemer Presbyterian Church in New York City, notes that although one's significance in modern society is less dependent on producing heirs, the pressure to find a partner persists. "Western culture tempts us to put our hopes in 'apocalyptic romance,' in finding complete spiritual and emotional fulfillment in the perfect mate. Innumerable Disney-style popular culture narratives begin telling life stories only when two parties are about to find True Love and then, once they do, the story fades out. The message is that what matters in life is finding romance and marriage. Everything else is prologue and afterword."[4]

This narrative is in tension with more recent notions. As early as the 1980s, Keller noticed shifting attitudes among his congregation's young urban professionals—attitudes that have since grown into mainstream objections to marriage: "Marriage crushes individual identity and has been oppressive for women, marriage stifles passion and is ill-fitted to psychological reality, marriage is 'just a piece of paper' that only serves to complicate love, and so on. But beneath these philosophical objections lies a snarl of conflicted personal emotions, born out of many negative experiences with marriage and family life."[5]

This chapter of *Restoring Relationships* inventories the relationships that connect people today within the context of broad cultural flux. Barna's findings confirm the pervasive problem of loneliness and highlight disparities in relational and emotional satisfaction between married people and singles, and between those with and without children. We also explore the benefits of frequent contact with family and loved ones, and examine how faith provides meaningful identity apart from marital and parental status—and how churches can play a role in combating loneliness.

Why is this so crucial? Because relationships are where the rubber of the gospel meets the road of everyday life. Christ came to redeem and restore lost and broken people, and our relationships are where redeemed, restored people live the good news. The Church can and must be a reliable place to turn for relational restoration.

To get the lay of the land, let's look first at the relationships people are in right now.

> Relationships are where the rubber of the gospel meets the road of everyday life. Christ came to redeem and restore lost and broken people, and our relationships are where redeemed, restored people live the good news

A CONSTELLATION OF RELATIONSHIPS

Researchers wanted to account for various relational realms, so the survey included questions about family of origin, current household, close friendships and trusted advisors, such as a pastor or professional counselor.

When it comes to family of origin, practicing Christians and U.S. adults overall are equally likely to have a living mother (58%). The proportions that have a living father also are the same (46% practicing Christians vs. 45% U.S. adults), less than half in both groups, but practicing Christians are slightly more likely to have a sibling (89% vs. 85%).

There are more significant differences when it comes to relationships that people make for themselves. Practicing Christians are much more likely to have a spouse (58% vs. 49%) and a child (68% vs. 59%). Among those 35 and older who have children, practicing Christians are also slightly more likely to have a grandchild (60% vs. 56%).

Outside the family, the overwhelming majority of both groups has close friends (95% vs. 91%). It's worth contemplating what this means: One in 20 practicing Christians and one in 10 U.S. adults say they do *not* have a close friend.

A Relationship Inventory, U.S. Adults vs. Practicing Christians

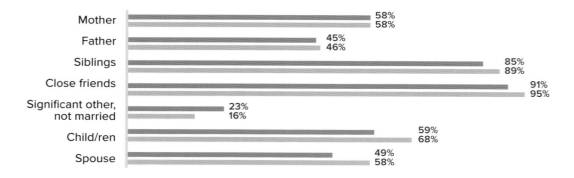

○ U.S. ADULTS
○ PRACTICING CHRISTIANS

Mother	58% / 58%
Father	45% / 46%
Siblings	85% / 89%
Close friends	91% / 95%
Significant other, not married	23% / 16%
Child/ren	59% / 68%
Spouse	49% / 58%

n = 2,307 U.S. adults 18 and over, March–May 2019.

Practicing Christians are more likely to have a counselor or therapist (25% vs. 20% all U.S. adults) and, unsurprisingly, almost twice as likely to have a pastor or priest (92% vs. 47%).

Marital Status

Although practicing Christians outpace the general population in being currently married, some aspects of marriage are similar across groups, including the age when first married. Among adults of any age who have ever been married, one's 20s, particularly the early- to mid-20s, is the most common age range for a first marriage; however, the average increases among each successively younger generation. Men tend to marry for the first time two to three years later than women. Teen marriages are less common (16% all adults) as are first-time spouses in their 30s (14%).

One in three practicing Christians who have ever been married has also been through a divorce (33%), slightly less than the 39 percent of all adults that have divorced. Widows and widowers are less common than divorcees, but they still make up a significant percentage of adults: Eight percent of all respondents' marriages ended with the death of a spouse.

Among practicing Christians who have ever been married, 33% have also been through a divorce, compared to 39% of all adults

Singleness

While the majority has been married, a sizeable number has not: One in four practicing Christians (26%) and one in three among all adults (35%) have never wed.

About one-third of these singles reports they are involved in a romantic relationship, with fewer couples among practicing Christian singles (31% vs. 37% of single U.S. adults). Similar percentages of singles are engaged (5% vs. 6%), in non-cohabitating serious relationships (9% all), dating (9% all) and not dating but looking (27% vs. 25%). Practicing Christian singles are less likely to be living with their significant other (8% vs. 14%).

More than half of Christian Millennials (55%) are single, significantly more than the percentage of singles in older Christian generations (between 35% and 40%). Some of the disparity is due to cultural norms surrounding marriageable age, and the more pronounced rise in singleness in the general population indicates the upward pressure on those norms: Millennials (70%) are far more likely than Gen X (48% single), Boomers (38%) and Elders (35%) to be single.

Practicing Christian Millennials are more likely than young adults in the general population to be married (45% vs. 30%)

Parenting ———

At first blush, the significantly higher percentage of practicing Christians who are parents (68% vs. 59% all adults) might indicate that practicing Christians are generally more open to having children. However, accounting only for people who are married, practicing Christians and the general population track closely when it comes to frequency of parenthood (84% vs. 82%, respectively).

Among those who have kids, the number of children and their ages are similar across both groups. Most are parents of two kids, followed by parents of a single child. One-fifth in both groups of parents has a toddler or infant (0–5 years). The percentage rises for those with school-aged children (6–12 years) while fewer have teens (13–18 years). Two-thirds of parents in both groups (65%) have an adult child (19+ years).

Number of Children

○ U.S. ADULTS
○ PRACTICING CHRISTIANS

None	One	Two	Three	Four	Five or more
41% 32%	18% 19%	22% 29%	12% 12%	5% 4%	2% 4%

n = 2,307 U.S. adults 18 and over, March–May 2019.

Ages of Children

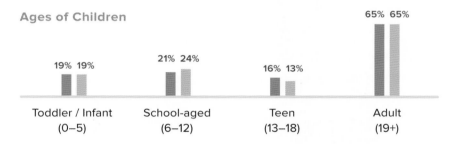

Toddler / Infant (0–5)	School-aged (6–12)	Teen (13–18)	Adult (19+)
19% 19%	21% 24%	16% 13%	65% 65%

n = 1,034 U.S. adults 18 and over with children, March–May 2019.

HOUSEHOLD COMPOSITION

Most people live in households comprised of a single generation (58% practicing Christians, 57% all)—that is, they do not live with their mother, father, sibling, children or grandchildren. Given the significant proportion of respondents with adult children, this is not surprising. Four out of five households of practicing Christians (80%) include a married couple, compared to two out of three households in the general population (66%). Seven percent of practicing Christian households include a cohabiting partner, half the percentage of the general population (14%).

The remaining households may include members of younger generations, children and / or grandchildren, as well as an older generation,

Continued on page 26.

THE AMBIGUOUS LOSS OF UNWANTED SINGLENESS

By Kelly Maxwell Haer, PhD

My father married at 23. My mother and my older sister married at 21. Growing up, I expected that my life would follow a similar course. I was painfully wrong.

I spent a dozen post-college years as a single person in the church. It was a mixed bag. On the good end, I remember my pastor asking me to review the transcript for his singleness sermon. I felt seen, recognized, included and respected. On the bad end, I remember many assurances from fellow congregants that God would bring me a special someone soon. I met my husband more than a decade after those assurances. Perhaps that was "soon" to God, but it sure didn't feel soon to me!

While many people may relate to my experience, there is no "typical" single. There is great variety. Though I deeply longed for a spouse, not everyone desires marriage. Some have never been married, whereas others are single again through divorce or death. Experiences differ by age and gender. Ministering to such a diverse, growing group of people can be challenging; it is critical not to make assumptions about any one single person.

One thing that's clear from the data, however, is that singles want to find help and refuge in their church as they navigate unpartnered life—so it's important that churches be ready to receive and relate to singles. Yet the data also suggest that pastors feel ill-equipped to address the challenges of singleness.

Where to begin this daunting task?

Understanding what it's like to be single is a good place to start. For singles who want to be married, the missing spouse is a type of ambiguous loss.* The longed-for partner, though physically absent, is alive in the minds of the hopeful, much as a spouse who is missing would be. It is difficult for singles to name, and thus hard to grieve, what is lost. This is partly because the partner could be found tomorrow—or never.

> There is no "typical" single. Ministering to such a diverse, growing group of people can be challenging—it is critical not to make assumptions about any one single person.

Because people often attend church with family, singles may feel the pain of ambiguous loss there more acutely than other places—such as the workplace, the gym or the grocery store—where people tend not to be with their families. Yet church can also be a place where that pain is endured and ultimately healed. Ambiguous loss can cause a single person to become frozen in one of the stages of grief or to rapidly cycle through them all. Corporate songs of lament became a refuge for me during my single years. I could bring my pain before God while surrounded by the Body of Christ.

Singles may wrestle with questions of identity and safety. *Why am I single? Is my singleness temporary or permanent? What can I do to find a spouse? How do people perceive me?* These questions are challenging because there is often no clear answer. But this lack of clarity offers an opportunity to seek identity and safety not in answers, but in Christ. As such, it is important not to rush to the rescue with clichés like "You're so great, I'm sure God will have someone for you soon," "It will happen when you least expect it" or "When you're satisfied and content God will bring someone into your life." Although well-meaning, these responses sometimes short circuit an uncomfortable process through which God is working. They can also alienate singles who feel missed, dismissed or generally not taken seriously. And, finally, they may communicate falsehoods. The single person doesn't know—and will never know—if God will bring them a spouse. And neither do you.

Better to say you don't know why God has allowed them to remain single, or when or if God might have a spouse for them. As unpleasant as these answers may be, they are honest and take pain seriously. Rather than dismissing the other person's pain, they draw you into it. Compassion means "to suffer with."

---

*My thanks to Dr. Pauline Boss for her groundbreaking work on the theory of ambiguous loss.

It isn't wrong to offer encouragement, but make sure it is rooted in biblical truth more than in statistical probabilities inferred from the experience of previous generations. You can encourage singles—or anyone, in fact—to find comfort in the lives of people like Joseph, Job and Paul, who lived in daily uncertainty, not knowing the outcome of their struggles.

> Make sure encouragement is rooted in biblical truth. Encourage singles to find comfort in the lives of people like Joseph, Job and Paul, who lived in daily uncertainty, not knowing the outcome of their struggles.

When praying for a single person who hopes to marry, it is better to pray that God would provide a spouse. Praying for a spouse as though certain that person exists, on the other hand, can heighten the feeling of ambiguous loss.

If you are married, fostering true friendship with singles, sharing the joys and sorrows of your life and marriage, will help them feel like they are more than a ministry project. And these genuine relationships will make it easier to include relevant, singles-oriented sermon illustrations! On an even more practical note,

having many single friends can position you to be a helpful matchmaker. And if you're genuinely acting as an interested friend, you'll be able to discern whether your friends would appreciate offers to set

KELLY HAER is the director of the Relationship IQ program at the Boone Center for the Family. She has a PhD in family therapy from Saint Louis University, a master's degree in counseling from Covenant Theological Seminary and a bachelor's degree from Furman University. Kelly has a wealth of experience working with singles in a variety of contexts, such as counseling sessions, the church community and research studies, including a project with eHarmony.

Check out the Boone Center for the Family website (www. boonecenter.pepperdine.edu) for resources on ministering to singles including a blog, an eBook chapter and a Quick Reference Guide.

them up or whether you're better off keeping your suggestions to yourself.

Seek communal ways to celebrate the significant events of your single friends' lives. Promotions, professional advancements, hobby achievements and sporting events are good opportunities to rally around the single person who is not celebrated within a marriage and family.

Don't allow singles without children to be invisible on Mother's and Father's Days. Many singles who long for marriage also long for children of their own. Of course, singles can adopt children, though many will not, given the demands of single parenting. Recognizing singleness as a type of infertility can be powerful and poignant.

Involving singles in church leadership can also help singles be seen and find belonging. My own ambiguous loss as a longtime single makes me especially thankful for how God has positioned me now: helping church leaders minister to singles through the RelateStrong Leadership Series at the Boone Center for the Family.

Continued from page 21.

such as a mother or father. Roughly half of parents have children living with them (49% practicing Christians, 52% all). Eleven percent of all parents from the practicing Christian group have a child over 18 living with them vs. 15 percent of the general population. Roughly one-fifth of respondents has a parent living with them (18% of practicing Christians vs. 21% all). A small minority of households includes grandchildren (3% vs. 2%).

KEEPING IN TOUCH

When people don't live in the same household, connecting with family and friends requires more effort. Overall, a robust majority of respondents is in weekly contact with loved ones outside their household, with practicing Christians more likely across the board to be in touch (88% vs. 82% all adults).

In Touch at Least Once a Week, U.S. Adults vs. Practicing Christians
(among those who have each relationship)

○ U.S. ADULTS
◌ PRACTICING CHRISTIANS

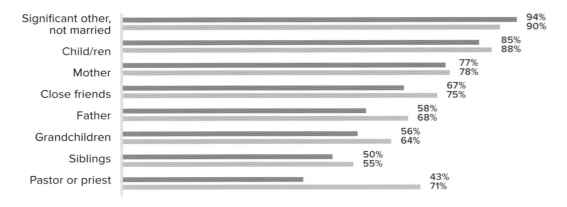

	U.S. Adults	Practicing Christians
Significant other, not married	94%	90%
Child/ren	85%	88%
Mother	77%	78%
Close friends	67%	75%
Father	58%	68%
Grandchildren	56%	64%
Siblings	50%	55%
Pastor or priest	43%	71%

n = 2,307 U.S. adults 18 and over, March–May 2019.

Outside the family unit, practicing Christians are more likely to be in touch weekly with a close friend (75% vs. 67% all). Weekly worship services and other regularly scheduled church activities likely facilitate some of these more frequent interactions.

Among those with a counselor or therapist, 26 percent of all adults and 29 percent of practicing Christians are in touch with their counselor once a week or more, but the most common frequency of contact is monthly (34% practicing Christians vs. 29% all). Although practicing Christians are far more likely to be in weekly contact with their pastor or priest (71%), a sizeable proportion of those in the general population who have a pastor (43%) also reports weekly contact.

RELATIONAL & EMOTIONAL SATISFACTION

As anyone in a relationship can testify, having one does not necessarily equal relational happiness—but it's a necessary start!

On the whole, emotional satisfaction is positive overall, but practicing Christians tend to report higher emotional satisfaction than the general population. They are more likely to generally feel loved (84% vs. 73% all), satisfied with their relationships (77% vs. 69%), satisfied with life (76% vs. 63%) and happy to be themselves (82% vs. 70%). They are also more likely to say that feelings of loneliness are infrequent (61% vs. 55%).

> Emotional satisfaction is generally positive, but practicing Christians, married people and parents tend to report greater well-being than U.S. adults overall, singles and people without children

Nevertheless, asymmetries in relationship satisfaction exist between subgroups, even among practicing Christians. Most notably, married people tend to be happier than singles and parents are generally more satisfied than those who don't have children.

Feelings Inventory, Married vs. Single

○ SINGLE U.S. ADULTS   ○ MARRIED U.S. ADULTS

"I ALWAYS OR USUALLY FEEL . . . "

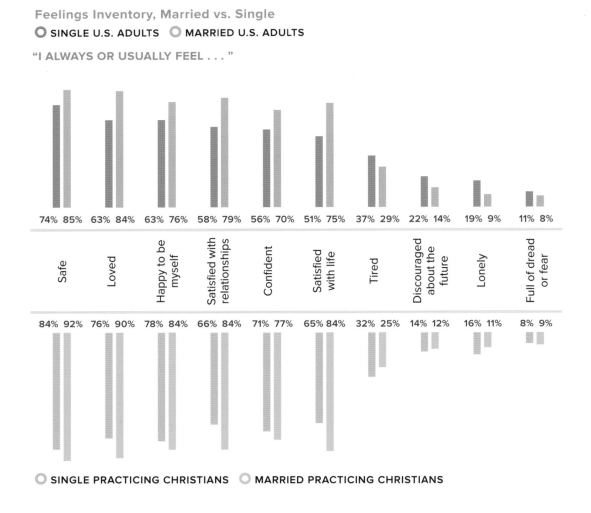

	Safe	Loved	Happy to be myself	Satisfied with relationships	Confident	Satisfied with life	Tired	Discouraged about the future	Lonely	Full of dread or fear
Single U.S. Adults	74%	63%	63%	58%	56%	51%	37%	22%	19%	11%
Married U.S. Adults	85%	84%	76%	79%	70%	75%	29%	14%	9%	8%
Single Practicing Christians	84%	76%	78%	66%	71%	65%	32%	14%	16%	8%
Married Practicing Christians	92%	90%	84%	84%	77%	84%	25%	12%	11%	9%

○ SINGLE PRACTICING CHRISTIANS   ○ MARRIED PRACTICING CHRISTIANS

n = 2,307 U.S. adults 18 and over, March–May 2019.

More than 20 years ago, Paige Benton Brown characterized the bulk of what had been written in Christian circles about singleness as stemming from a pervasive attitude that singles "bear the cross of 'Plan B' for the Christian life."[6] Brown, by contrast, sought to place her identity in her redemptive status rather than her marital status, and to celebrate her singleness at the time as God's best for her. Brown also noted that the range of human relationships extends beyond the marriage relationship, and that "Christian growth mandates relational richness."

Although Brown's essay encouraged a paradigm realignment for singleness, old mindsets change slowly; a comparison of the responses of single practicing Christians to their married counterparts indicates there is still room for churches' growth in meeting their felt needs. Single practicing Christians are more likely than married practicing Christians to admit they are dissatisfied with their relationships (13% vs. 4%), and to say depression (38% vs. 29%), loneliness (36% vs. 24%) and grief (30% vs. 22%) affect their most important relationships. Singles are also less likely to have a positive experience with a church as a help source when they turned to a church leader during a difficult situation (77% vs. 87%). Curiously, single practicing Christians are more likely than their married counterparts to attend a church where they never hear leaders talk about marriage (20% vs. 8%), singleness (52% vs. 43%) or parenting (24% vs. 16%). When their church leaders address difficult or sensitive issues, such as addiction or sexual intimacy, singles are less likely to find the church's efforts to be helpful (49% vs. 68%). Overall, single practicing Christians are less optimistic in their expectations of the Church being a source of help for navigating relational difficulties (78% vs. 84%).

A comparison of single practicing Christians to their married counterparts indicates there is room for churches' growth in meeting singles' felt needs. If they know relational help is available, they are likely to take advantage of it.

That being said, they are just as likely as married practicing Christians to say they would prefer to go to a pastor or priest in a time of personal crisis, with two in five placing a pastor / priest in their top three sources of help (39% vs. 38% of married practicing Christians). This signals a meaningful opportunity for churches: If singles know relational help is available to unmarried people, they are likely to take advantage of it.

Churches sometimes unconsciously (or even consciously) communicate a hierarchy that puts "married with children" at the pinnacle of value. That's unfortunate, because practicing Christians without children (78%) are already less likely than practicing Christian parents to report an abiding sense of being loved (87%) and to be satisfied with their relationships (71% vs. 79%). They are more likely to frequently feel lonely than those with children (20% vs. 11%), and to say that depression (38% vs. 31%), loneliness (34% vs. 26%) and anxiety (42% vs. 34%) affect their most important relationships. Childless practicing Christians are also less likely to include a pastor or priest among the top three most preferred people to turn to for help with a personal crisis (34% vs. 41%) and less likely to hold an optimistic overall expectation of a church being a source of help for relationship struggles (77% vs. 83%).

If they have actually experienced a church's help, however, practicing Christians without children are equally likely to have had a positive experience as practicing Christians with children. Again, this signifies an open door for churches that are prepared to give relationship guidance to people who are hungry for help, but may not look like a church's "ideal" nuclear family.

Practicing Christian parents enjoy numerous positives, including (perhaps unexpectedly) less relational strain: Those without kids are more likely to acknowledge marriage problems affect their most important relationships (33% vs. 24% of practicing Christian parents).

There is encouraging news: Both single practicing Christians and childless practicing Christians have consistently higher rates of emotional and relational satisfaction than their counterparts in the general population. Singles who are practicing Christians are more likely than other singles to feel loved (76% vs. 63%), satisfied with their relationships (65% vs. 58%) and satisfied with life (66% vs. 51%). Similarly, those without children who are practicing Christians are also more likely than their counterparts to feel loved (78% vs. 66%), satisfied with their relationships (71% vs. 61%) and satisfied with life (70% vs. 55%).

> Both single and childless practicing Christians have consistently higher rates of emotional and relational satisfaction than their counterparts in the general population—which may indicate that churches are moving in the right direction

This may indicate that churches are taking to heart reminders of the early Church's emphasis on community fellowship or affirmation of singleness and are moving in the right direction. Teaching on belonging to a spiritual family and dedicating one's life to a missional vocation may likewise buffer practicing Christians from some of the negative aspects of being childless.

When it comes to frequent feelings of loneliness, however, singles and the childless in both groups respond similarly (16% practicing Christian singles vs. 19% all U.S. singles, 20% childless practicing Christians vs. 18% all U.S. adults without children), which signals an area for Christian communities to address. The weekly rhythms of church life are one solution, as there is a strong correlation between frequent contact with loved ones and being satisfied relationally. Practicing Christians who say they are usually or always satisfied with their relationships are significantly more likely to have weekly contact with loved ones (89%) than those who say they're dissatisfied with their relationships (81%).

Continued on page 35.

A CHURCH FAMILY FOR YOUNG ADULTS (& EVERYONE ELSE)

A Q&A with Katelyn Beaty

Q.

Career development and vocation are a top priority for a lot of young adults, often more so than marriage and parenting. How can churches keep this in mind as they minister to and support young adults? What does it look like to nurture the relational or mental health of these groups, whose identity may stem from their title, or whose community might center around their workplace?

A.

Churches must provide a robust theology of work and vocation that prioritizes work done in the "secular" world as much as work done in the world of formal ministry. Churches can help young adults see their workplaces as seedbeds of personal and kingdom transformation. Many young adults are searching for meaning in their daily work—they want to know that their work "matters." Churches can provide young adults with a theological framework for understanding the spiritual meaning of their work, even and especially when that work seems rote or unglamorous.

A church family can also be helpful when it comes to navigating relationships outside the immediate family. For instance, if we are working a full-time job, it typically means we are spending more waking hours with our coworkers than with anyone else, often including our families. Workplace relationships have a profound effect on our well-being. Church leaders can provide tools that help us manage conflict, communicate well and build trust in *any* important relationship in our lives.

Churches can also help ambitious young adults find their ultimate identity in who God says they are, not in what they do and accomplish. That comes from faithfully preaching the gospel and from creating communities where people are celebrated for who they are, not what they do.

Q.

Barna has found evidence across a number of studies that young adults, especially young women, are struggling with feelings of loneliness, disconnection and isolation. What are some ways that churches could help young women, whatever their family situation, to experience a deeper sense of community?

A.

One obvious answer is simply to create community—to offer plenty of opportunities for women in various life stages to connect with each other through deep conversation, fun and rest. The local church can be a primary place for young adults to find connection in the midst of changes in job, location and relationship status, especially in their early- to mid-20s, when life feels very in flux.

But the loneliness and isolation that many young women experience probably won't be solved by one-off church events. We have to address the ways that digital technology isolates many young people, including Christians, from real connection, even as it makes us *feel* more connected than ever. Churches can provide theological resources and spiritual tools that keep technology in its proper place, and that create opportunity for in-the-flesh connection and community.

Q.

Married adults are more likely than singles to report feeling loved, safe, satisfied with life and relationships, happy "to be myself" and confident, while singles are more prone to negative feelings like loneliness and discouragement about the future. How can churches help singles fill the gap? What should single Christians ask of their faith community?

A.

Churches have a crucial role to play in providing a positive and life-giving narrative of singleness, one that emphasizes its blessings and freedoms. This is a core biblical principle, but unfortunately, many single Christians, myself included, have experienced a Christian subculture that envisions marriage and family as the highest or best calling. Instead, churches can teach that no one life situation is better than the other, that each has its unique blessings and challenges.

Single Christians should ask their faith communities to make sure they are visible in church leadership. If all of the visible leaders in a church community are married with kids, that can unhelpfully reinforce the notion that marriage and family are required for effective ministry—but Jesus and Paul seem to think differently.

KATELYN BEATY is author of *A Woman's Place: A Christian Vision for Your Calling in the Office, the Home, and the World*. She speaks regularly on professional work, singleness and women's issues. Learn more at KatelynBeaty.com.

Continued from page 31.

Yet, according to social neuroscientist Dr. John Cacioppo, "To end loneliness, you need other people—plus something else. You also need . . . to feel you are sharing something with the other person, or the group, that is meaningful to both of you. . . . Loneliness isn't the physical absence of other people—it's the sense that you're not sharing anything that matters with anyone else."[7] Beyond providing opportunity for human contact, churches are places of shared meaning. Churches can and should be places where the gospel is embodied, where the grace of God overshadows whether one is married or single, a parent or childless, or any other relational distinction.

With that in mind, let's take stock of the relationships people say are most in need.

VISUALIZING THE ISSUES
DIVING DEEP INTO THE PLACES PEOPLE ARE STRUGGLING TODAY

It can be hard to tell from the outside what relational and emotional burdens people are carrying around with them to work, to school, to the grocery store—and to church. So Barna researchers asked! This special data visualization section is a dive into the relational deep end, where many people are tiring out, treading water or looking for a life preserver.

Across the nation, more than half of all adults and practicing Christians report at least one relational or emotional health issue—like marital or parenting problems, depression, addiction or loneliness—that impacts their most significant relationships. Half of those say they are struggling with not just one but two or more such problems.

% among people who report at least one relational or emotional health issue that impacts their most important relationships

58%

U.S. ADULTS

54%

PRACTICING CHRISTIANS

RISING CHALLENGES

What are the specific issues at work in people's everyday lives? In consultation with pastors and mental health clinicians, we offered survey participants a list of common problems and asked them to rate the impact of each one on their most important relationships. Here are the percentages of U.S. adults and practicing Christians who are caught in the current of relational upheaval.

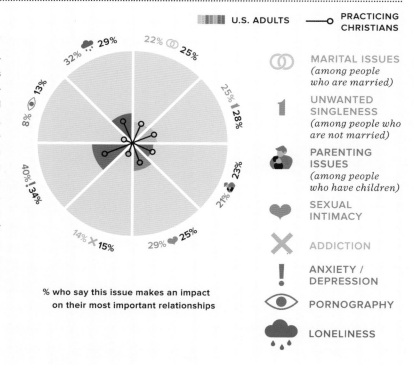

░░░ U.S. ADULTS   ⊸ PRACTICING CHRISTIANS

29% 🌧 32%
22% ◎ 25%
25% | 28%
23% 👣 21%
25% ♥ 29%
14% ✕ 15%
40% | 34%
8% 👁 13%

% who say this issue makes an impact on their most important relationships

MARITAL ISSUES *(among people who are married)*

UNWANTED SINGLENESS *(among people who are not married)*

PARENTING ISSUES *(among people who have children)*

SEXUAL INTIMACY

ADDICTION

ANXIETY / DEPRESSION

PORNOGRAPHY

LONELINESS

EBBING SATISFACTION

People who are struggling with even one of these eight issues in their relationships report lower satisfaction in their relationships and with life in general. For example, just two-thirds of these practicing Christians (67%) are satisfied with their relationships, compared to nine out of 10 who aren't contending with the relational impact of any of these challenges.

"I always or usually feel…"

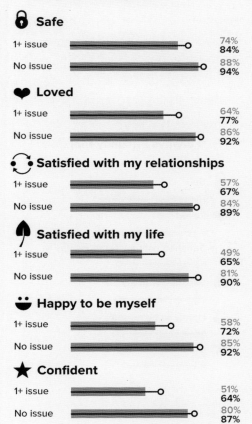

🔒 **Safe**

1+ issue	74% / 84%
No issue	88% / 94%

♥ **Loved**

1+ issue	64% / 77%
No issue	86% / 92%

🔄 **Satisfied with my relationships**

1+ issue	57% / 67%
No issue	84% / 89%

🌱 **Satisfied with my life**

1+ issue	49% / 65%
No issue	81% / 90%

😃 **Happy to be myself**

1+ issue	58% / 72%
No issue	85% / 92%

★ **Confident**

1+ issue	51% / 64%
No issue	80% / 87%

RIPPLE EFFECTS

The next few pages take an up-close look at each of these relational or emotional challenges. Here's what you'll find for each one:

- A demographic profile of people who are facing that particular issue. This can help you know who in your community is most likely to need help.
- A bar chart that shows how their struggle may be impacting their overall satisfaction and sense of well-being.
- A wheel image, like the one on the opposite page, to help you visualize how dealing with that issue ripples into other areas of life. This vividly demonstrates one of this study's most important takeaways: Relational and emotional problems often go hand in hand. A person who is struggling with compulsive pornography use, for example, is more likely also to face marital problems.

Understanding the real issues people are dealing with is the first step toward restoration.

MARITAL PROBLEMS
IMPACT MY MOST IMPORTANT RELATIONSHIPS

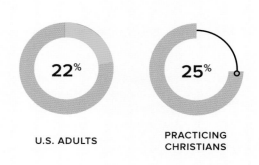

22%
U.S. ADULTS

25%
PRACTICING CHRISTIANS

GENDER			
Male		19%	26%
Female		25%	25%
AGE*			
Millennials		23%	43%
Gen X		27%	32%
Boomers		21%	15%
RELATIONSHIP STATUS			
Previously divorced		28%	34%
Parent		24%	24%
Child 18 or under		29%	38%
Child 19+		21%	15%
No children		15%	33%
FAITH IDENTITY			
Protestant		20%	25%
Catholic		20%	27%
No faith		27%	n/a

I'M ALSO FACING THESE OTHER CHALLENGES

% impacted by marital problems who say this issue also makes an impact on their most important relationships

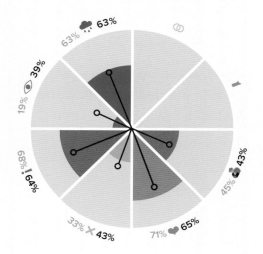

63% 63%
39%
19%
68% 64%
33% 43%
71% 65%
45% 43%

MARITAL ISSUES
UNWANTED SINGLENESS
PARENTING ISSUES
SEXUAL INTIMACY
ADDICTION
ANXIETY / DEPRESSION
PORNOGRAPHY
LONELINESS

HERE'S HOW IT IMPACTS MY SENSE OF WELL-BEING

"I always / usually feel..."

Safe — 68% / 84%

Loved — 58% / 80%

Satisfied with my relationships — 47% / 67%

Satisfied with my life — 45% / 67%

Happy to be myself — 53% / 70%

Confident — 50% / 63%

* Sample sizes in this study for Gen Z and Elders are too small to separately analyze.

UNWANTED SINGLENESS

IMPACTS MY MOST IMPORTANT RELATIONSHIPS

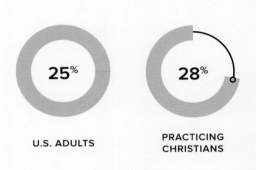

25% U.S. ADULTS

28% PRACTICING CHRISTIANS

GENDER			
Male		29%	30%
Female		22%	26%
AGE			
Millennials		32%	36%
Gen X		24%	32%
Boomers		22%	19%
RELATIONSHIP STATUS			
Never married		29%	30%
Ever divorced		19%	24%
Single parent		25%	28%
Child 18 or under		30%	37%
Child 19+		22%	22%
No children		25%	27%
FAITH IDENTITY			
Protestant		26%	30%
Catholic		23%	15%
No faith		23%	n/a

I'M ALSO FACING THESE OTHER CHALLENGES

% impacted by unwanted singleness who say this issue also makes an impact on their most important relationships

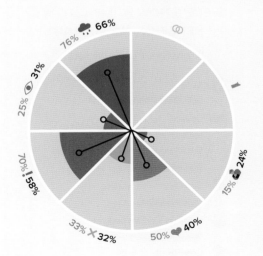

MARITAL ISSUES
UNWANTED SINGLENESS
PARENTING ISSUES
SEXUAL INTIMACY
ADDICTION
ANXIETY / DEPRESSION
PORNOGRAPHY
LONELINESS

HERE'S HOW IT IMPACTS MY SENSE OF WELL-BEING

"I always / usually feel..."

Safe — 60% / 78%
Loved — 48% / 65%
Satisfied with my relationships — 40% / 50%
Satisfied with my life — 35% / 54%
Happy to be myself — 49% / 67%
Confident — 45% / 63%

PARENTING ISSUES
IMPACT MY MOST IMPORTANT RELATIONSHIPS

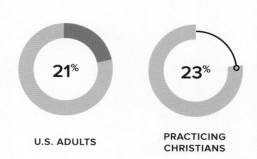

21%
U.S. ADULTS

23%
PRACTICING CHRISTIANS

GENDER		
Male	20%	25%
Female	22%	22%
AGE		
Millennials	35%	39%
Gen X	28%	30%
Boomers	14%	16%
RELATIONSHIP STATUS		
Currently married	20%	23%
Ever divorced	24%	27%
Single parent	24%	24%
Have child 0–5	36%	38%
Have child 6–12	28%	36%
Have child 13–18	35%	34%
Child 18 or under	31%	35%
Child 19+	15%	16%
FAITH IDENTITY		
Protestant	19%	23%
Catholic	19%	22%
No faith	28%	n/a

I'M ALSO FACING THESE OTHER CHALLENGES

% impacted by parenting issues who say this issue also makes an impact on their most important relationships

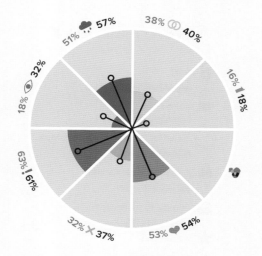

57%
51%
38% 40%
32%
18% 16% 18%
63% 61%
32% 37%
53% 54%

◖◗ MARITAL ISSUES
❗ UNWANTED SINGLENESS
👪 PARENTING ISSUES
💜 SEXUAL INTIMACY

✖ ADDICTION
❗ ANXIETY / DEPRESSION
👁 PORNOGRAPHY
☁ LONELINESS

HERE'S HOW IT IMPACTS MY SENSE OF WELL-BEING

"I always / usually feel..."

🔒 **Safe**
67%
83%

💜 **Loved**
65%
77%

🔄 **Satisfied with my relationships**
56%
62%

🍃 **Satisfied with my life**
47%
62%

😃 **Happy to be myself**
54%
67%

⭐ **Confident**
50%
60%

PROBLEMS WITH SEXUAL INTIMACY

IMPACT MY MOST IMPORTANT RELATIONSHIPS

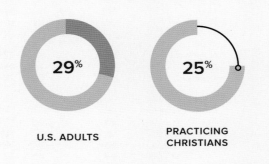

29% U.S. ADULTS

25% PRACTICING CHRISTIANS

GENDER			
Male		27%	27%
Female		31%	23%
AGE			
Millennials		31%	31%
Gen X		29%	27%
Boomers		29%	20%
RELATIONSHIP STATUS			
Currently married		33%	28%
Single		26%	20%
Ever divorced		36%	29%
Parent		30%	25%
Child 18 or under		38%	32%
Child 19+		28%	21%
Non-parent		28%	24%
FAITH IDENTITY			
Protestant		27%	25%
Catholic		30%	26%
No faith		30%	n/a

I'M ALSO FACING THESE OTHER CHALLENGES

% impacted by problems with sexual intimacy who say this issue also makes an impact on their most important relationships

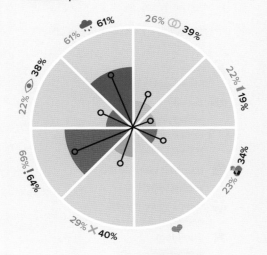

- 26% ⊕ 39%
- 22% ▌ 19%
- 34%
- 23% 🦋
- 29% ✗ 40%
- 66% ▌64%
- 22% 👁 38%
- 61% 🌧 61%

ⓘ MARITAL ISSUES ✗ ADDICTION
1 UNWANTED SINGLENESS ! ANXIETY / DEPRESSION
👤 PARENTING ISSUES 👁 PORNOGRAPHY
♥ SEXUAL INTIMACY 🌧 LONELINESS

HERE'S HOW IT IMPACTS MY SENSE OF WELL-BEING

"I always / usually feel..."

🔒 **Safe**
72%
83%

♥ **Loved**
61%
75%

🔄 **Satisfied with my relationships**
53%
62%

🍃 **Satisfied with my life**
45%
61%

😀 **Happy to be myself**
57%
70%

★ **Confident**
49%
50%

ADDICTION
IMPACTS MY MOST IMPORTANT RELATIONSHIPS

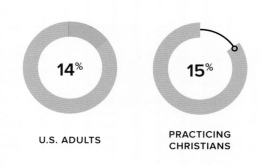

14%
U.S. ADULTS

15%
PRACTICING CHRISTIANS

GENDER			
Male		15%	21%
Female		13%	10%
AGE			
Millennials		19%	27%
Gen X		17%	19%
Boomers		10%	7%
RELATIONSHIP STATUS			
Currently married		10%	14%
Single		17%	17%
Ever divorced		17%	17%
Parent		13%	14%
Child 18 or under		18%	23%
Child 19+		10%	8%
Non-parent		15%	17%
FAITH IDENTITY			
Protestant		13%	15%
Catholic		15%	14%
No faith		12%	n/a

I'M ALSO FACING THESE OTHER CHALLENGES

% impacted by addiction who say this issue also makes an impact on their most important relationships

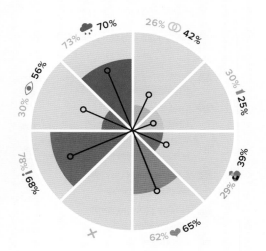

MARITAL ISSUES
UNWANTED SINGLENESS
PARENTING ISSUES
SEXUAL INTIMACY
ADDICTION
ANXIETY / DEPRESSION
PORNOGRAPHY
LONELINESS

HERE'S HOW IT IMPACTS MY SENSE OF WELL-BEING

"I always / usually feel..."

Safe — 64% / 77%
Loved — 54% / 71%
Satisfied with my relationships — 46% / 62%
Satisfied with my life — 39% / 59%
Happy to be myself — 47% / 68%
Confident — 43% / 62%

ANXIETY OR DEPRESSION
IMPACTS MY MOST IMPORTANT RELATIONSHIPS

40%
U.S. ADULTS

34%
PRACTICING CHRISTIANS

GENDER			
Male		36%	31%
Female		44%	36%
AGE			
Millennials		56%	45%
Gen X		39%	39%
Boomers		32%	26%
RELATIONSHIP STATUS			
Currently married		33%	32%
Single		47%	36%
Ever divorced		44%	39%
Parent		38%	33%
Child 18 or under		49%	46%
Child 19+		30%	25%
Non-parent		44%	36%
FAITH IDENTITY			
Protestant		38%	35%
Catholic		33%	28%
No faith		50%	n/a

I'M ALSO FACING THESE OTHER CHALLENGES

% impacted by anxiety or depression who say this issue also makes an impact on their most important relationships

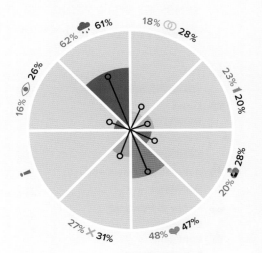

MARITAL ISSUES
UNWANTED SINGLENESS
PARENTING ISSUES
SEXUAL INTIMACY
ADDICTION
ANXIETY / DEPRESSION
PORNOGRAPHY
LONELINESS

HERE'S HOW IT IMPACTS MY SENSE OF WELL-BEING

"I always / usually feel…"

Safe — 69% / 80%
Loved — 58% / 74%
Satisfied with my relationships — 52% / 62%
Satisfied with my life — 39% / 57%
Happy to be myself — 49% / 66%
Confident — 42% / 55%

PORNOGRAPHY
IMPACTS MY MOST IMPORTANT RELATIONSHIPS

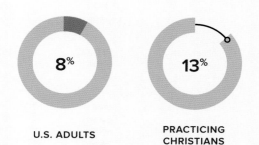

8%

U.S. ADULTS

13%

PRACTICING CHRISTIANS

GENDER			
Male		11%	20%
Female		5%	7%
AGE			
Millennials		12%	26%
Gen X		10%	17%
Boomers		5%	4%
RELATIONSHIPS			
Currently married		6%	13%
Single		10%	13%
Ever divorced		8%	12%
Parent		6%	11%
Child 18 or under		8%	21%
Child 19+		4%	4%
Non-parent		12%	17%
FAITH IDENTITY			
Protestant		8%	13%
Catholic		8%	12%
No faith		7%	n/a

I'M ALSO FACING THESE OTHER CHALLENGES

% impacted by pornography or sexual addiction who say this issue also makes an impact on their most important relationships

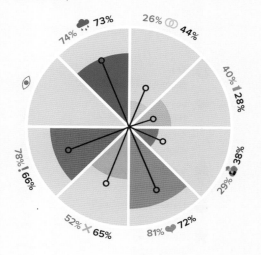

73%
74%   26% 44%
40% 28%
38%
29%
81% 72%
52% 65%
78% 66%

◐ **MARITAL ISSUES**   ✗ **ADDICTION**
❗ **UNWANTED SINGLENESS**   ❗ **ANXIETY / DEPRESSION**
👤 **PARENTING ISSUES**   👁 **PORNOGRAPHY**
💜 **SEXUAL INTIMACY**   🌧 **LONELINESS**

HERE'S HOW IT IMPACTS MY SENSE OF WELL-BEING

"I always / usually feel..."

🔒 **Safe**
59%
78%

💜 **Loved**
54%
72%

🔄 **Satisfied with my relationships**
49%
66%

🌿 **Satisfied with my life**
38%
59%

😃 **Happy to be myself**
54%
70%

⭐ **Confident**
50%
61%

LONELINESS
IMPACTS MY MOST IMPORTANT RELATIONSHIPS

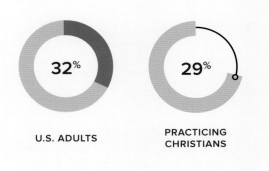

32% U.S. ADULTS

29% PRACTICING CHRISTIANS

GENDER			
Male		29%	30%
Female		35%	28%
AGE			
Millennials:		43%	39%
Gen X		35%	35%
Boomers		25%	20%
RELATIONSHIPS			
Currently married		22%	24%
Single		42%	36%
Ever divorced		33%	33%
Parent		30%	26%
Child 18 or under		36%	38%
Child 19+		26%	19%
Non-parnet		35%	34%
FAITH IDENTITY			
Protestant		31%	30%
Catholic		28%	23%
No faith		38%	n/a

I'M ALSO FACING THESE OTHER CHALLENGES

% impacted by loneliness who say this issue also makes an impact on their most important relationships

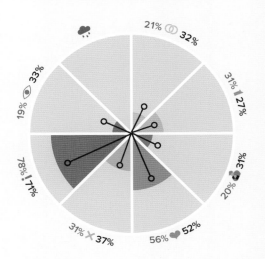

- 21% / 32% (marital issues)
- 33% / 19% (pornography)
- 31% / 27% (unwanted singleness)
- 31% (parenting issues)
- 20% / 31% (parenting issues)
- 78% / 71% (anxiety / depression)
- 31% / 37% (addiction)
- 56% / 52% (sexual intimacy)

MARITAL ISSUES   ADDICTION
UNWANTED SINGLENESS   ANXIETY / DEPRESSION
PARENTING ISSUES   PORNOGRAPHY
SEXUAL INTIMACY   LONELINESS

HERE'S HOW IT IMPACTS MY SENSE OF WELL-BEING

"I always / usually feel..."

- Safe — 67% / 79%
- Loved — 48% / 67%
- Satisfied with my relationships — 42% / 55%
- Satisfied with my life — 34% / 52%
- Happy to be myself — 45% / 62%
- Confident — 41% / 56%

2

HOW ARE RELATIONSHIPS UNDER PRESSURE?

When we're not suffering, it can be easier to recognize the important role suffering plays in preparing us and our relationships to receive God's grace—but it's much harder when we're in the midst of hardship and pain. This chapter explores "the midst," the places where people say they are feeling acute relational pressure. The question underlying all these data points is this: *How can churches help people receive grace where their relationships need it most?*

PRESSURE POINTS

Researchers compiled a list of common problems and asked respondents to evaluate the impact of each on their relationships. Roughly one in four among U.S. adults (25%) and practicing Christians (28%) reports no relational impact from any of the problems—which means three out of four people are feeling pressure of some kind in their relationships.

Three out of four people are experiencing relational pressure of some kind

Two in five U.S. adults and one-third of practicing Christians report they are dealing with anxiety or depression that has an impact on their significant relationships. Research participants were asked to indicate the degree to which pressures such as marriage problems, parenting problems, issues with sexual intimacy, addiction, pornography, anxiety, depression, loneliness and grief affect their relationships. Most do not perceive these as issues that make an impact. However, significant minorities indicate that anxiety (42% all U.S.

Issues That Make an Impact on My Relationships, U.S. Adults vs. Practicing Christians

○ U.S. ADULTS
○ PRACTICING CHRISTIANS

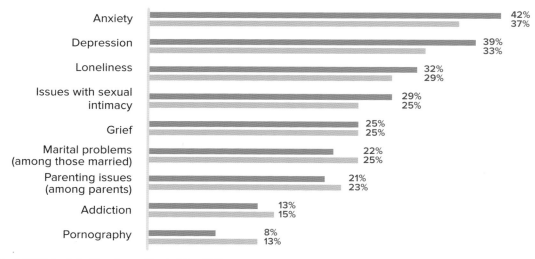

	U.S. Adults	Practicing Christians
Anxiety	42%	37%
Depression	39%	33%
Loneliness	32%	29%
Issues with sexual intimacy	29%	25%
Grief	25%	25%
Marital problems (among those married)	22%	25%
Parenting issues (among parents)	21%	23%
Addiction	13%	15%
Pornography	8%	13%

n = 2,307 U.S. adults 18 and over, March–May 2019.

adults), depression (39%), loneliness (32%), issues with sexual intimacy (29%), marriage problems (25%) and grief (25%) do have an effect. Parenting problems (21%) are present but less widespread, while addiction (13%) and pornography (8%) are the least frequently reported relational issues.

As the chart shows, similar proportions of practicing Christians report relational difficulties in these areas. Notably, Christians are more likely than the general population to consider pornography a problem. This may be because porn, until very recently, has been less taboo in the wider culture than in the Christian community; among Christians, as we'll see below, it's still considered quite serious.

Researchers asked senior pastors what issues they believe their parishioners often deal with. On the whole, their assessments indicate deep pastoral concern.

Issues That Make an Impact on Congregants' Relationships, U.S. Pastors / Priests

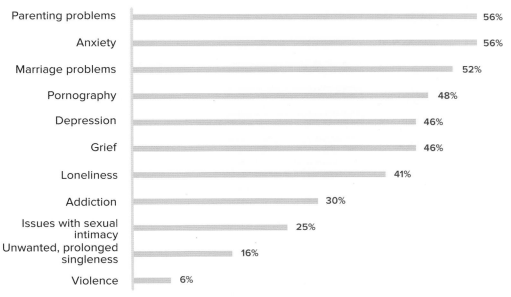

Parenting problems	56%
Anxiety	56%
Marriage problems	52%
Pornography	48%
Depression	46%
Grief	46%
Loneliness	41%
Addiction	30%
Issues with sexual intimacy	25%
Unwanted, prolonged singleness	16%
Violence	6%

n = 656 U.S. Protestant senior pastors and Catholic priests, March–April 2019.

THE RIPPLE EFFECTS OF RELATIONAL TRAUMA

Relationship pressures are rarely isolated and, in fact, tend to compound. As we might expect, the relational issues explored above emerge in greater proportions among U.S. adults and practicing Christians who have experienced relational trauma of some kind, including cheating / infidelity, depression / anxiety, addiction, pornography or sexual addiction, or another traumatic event (health problems, abuse, incarceration, miscarriage and so on), compared to those who have no experience with each type of trauma. In fact, overall relationship satisfaction is highest (89%) among those who have never personally experienced or had a loved one who has experienced relational trauma—and satisfaction is lower (66%) for those who report some kind of trauma either directly or through a loved one.

Feelings Inventory, by Experience of Trauma
○ **ANY TRAUMA** ○ **NO TRAUMA**

"I ALWAYS OR OFTEN FEEL . . . "

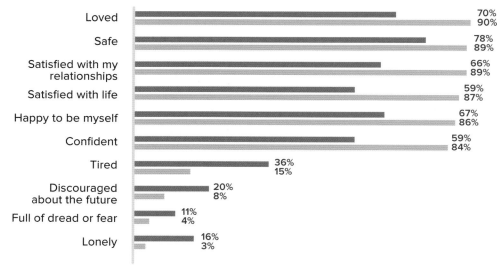

	ANY TRAUMA	NO TRAUMA
Loved	70%	90%
Safe	78%	89%
Satisfied with my relationships	66%	89%
Satisfied with life	59%	87%
Happy to be myself	67%	86%
Confident	59%	84%
Tired	36%	15%
Discouraged about the future	20%	8%
Full of dread or fear	11%	4%
Lonely	16%	3%

n = 2,307 U.S. adults 18 and over, March–May 2019.

Depression / Anxiety ————

As noted above, anxiety and depression are the most widely reported relational issues—due at least in part to the increasing ease people feel with discussing mental health—and these are most likely to surface among those who have direct experience of trauma. For example, just seven percent of U.S. adults with no personal experience of depression / anxiety indicate that depression affects their relationships, compared to two-thirds of those who have experienced depression / anxiety themselves (65%). Similarly, only one in nine of those with no personal experience (11%) says anxiety affects their relationships, while two-thirds of those who have experienced depression / anxiety (67%) say so. Depression / anxiety is also linked to higher reports of loneliness (49% vs. 10% of those with no experience) and grief (38% vs. 8%) as relational issues.

> Anxiety and depression are the most widely reported relational issues—due at least in part to the increasing ease people feel with discussing mental health

Trauma need not be personally experienced for its effects to be felt in a relationship. The effects of trauma ripple outward. Having a spouse, child or other loved one who has suffered the experience has at least as much of an effect, and sometimes even more. For instance, just eight percent of adults with no experience of depression / anxiety report marital problems, compared to one-third (37%) of those who have personally experienced depression / anxiety and one-third (35%) of those whose loved one has experienced depression / anxiety.

Pornography & Sexual Addiction ————

Although pornography and sexual addiction are the least reported of the traumas considered in the study, their effect on relationships appears to be among the most damaging. (Keep in mind that researchers

Continued on page 56.

HELPING YOUNG PEOPLE INTO HEALTHY RELATIONSHIPS

A Q&A with Michael Cox

Q.

What relational skills do you think are essential for adolescents to practice at home and beyond? How can churches and youth ministry be a part of their relational development?

A.

First, authentic engagement. Both home and church should be safe places for young people to express themselves without judgment or fear.

If young people are unable to be real in the two places that are supposed to be safe—home and church—they're going to find somewhere else. Unfortunately, that place may not be biblical or safe. They may just find someone to affirm or reinforce their thoughts, whether those thoughts are good or bad.

Second, listening without judgment. Teens need to feel listened to, and they need to learn to listen well. Part of good communication is learning how to hear with the right level of filtering. *What's important? What's not? How can I tell? Who do I listen to, who do I not listen to?*

Churches can create spaces where it's safe to ask questions, to explore, to engage in different and difficult topics in order to gain understanding around those things—and not feel judged. We don't have to affirm or confirm everyone's viewpoint, but we do want them to know it's safe to ask, to raise those questions, and have an authentic exchange.

The third thing is modeling. Young people are developing their viewpoint, their worldview, their faith. All those things are in a hyper mode of development and can really be shaped by engagement with adults who model authenticity and humility, who own their mistakes, communicate with grace and relate in healthy ways.

Q.

What factors do you believe lie behind the uptick in anxiety and depression among teens and young adults? What are some ways that pastors and youth ministry workers can help young people navigate mental illness?

A.

I think three main factors are at work. The first is access to information. Literally at their fingertips, young people have a way to find out more about what they're experiencing. And that's great, as long as they're getting good information.

Second, general awareness and cultural conversation. We talk more about mental illness now than in the past. In addition to face-to-face conversations, teens are bombarded by YouTube, Snapchat, podcasts, all these things where mental illness is just a normal topic.

Third, and related to that, is that anxiety and depression are kind of trendy. Talking about it is another opportunity to relate and connect, everybody bands together around that issue. Doesn't mean it's not legitimate, but it's easier for folks to grab onto because anxiety and depression are kind of the thing to do right now.

The acknowledgement that mental health problems are real is a huge, important place for church leaders to start. It can be damaging, both emotionally and spiritually, for someone to grow up in a space where experiencing mental illness is chalked up to a lack of faith.

The second way to help is for pastors and youth leaders to get informed. Whether it's through education, through partnerships, through literature, through whatever—get informed about what mental health problems are and what the symptoms look like.

The last thing is for ministry workers to recognize when they've reached the limits of their training and abilities. If a young person comes to them with a problem, I think it's healthy for a leader to say, "I don't have the training to help you through this process. Let's partner with someone who does. I can walk with you, I can pray with you, I can support you, but this is something beyond my know-how."

Q.

Pornography and sexual imagery have become ubiquitous in our culture. In your own counseling practice, how have you seen these affect teens and families? What can churches do to help young people develop healthy sexuality and Christian sexual ethics?

A.

Exposure is happening earlier than in the past. Access, again. It's at their fingertips. On top of that, I see a lot of ignorance or a lack of sensitivity about how porn will affect them over the long term. They see it as not that big of a deal, "everyone else is doing it," or it's just natural.

A lot of times, a true, authentic conversation with family members isn't happening. Often parents aren't sure what to say to their teen about what's happening, so rather than talk about it they just put down hard-and-fast rules without talking about why the guidelines are so important.

The truth is, sometimes it's not just a problem for young people. It's a problem for adults, too. Their parents, their teachers, their pastors. So you have adults who are struggling in this area, and they're like, "How can I lead that conversation? Because it's my problem too."

Church leadership and parents can start early to establish safe environments

MICHAEL COX is a Level 2 Certified Restoration Therapist. Together with his wife, Coloma, he conducts marriage seminars, coaches couples in preparation for marriage and walks with families seeking to live healthy lives. Additionally, Michael utilizes his 20+ years of working with young people to inform and drive his work with adolescent development and emotional regulation. He is a trainer in Mental Health First Aid for the National Council for Behavioral Health, and he lives in Texas with his wife and three children.

where young people can talk openly and ask honest questions about sex. Open the door, even if it's painful and awkward, to an authentic conversation about what they're experiencing. Don't shame them for having desires. Instead, help them understand healthy and God-ordered ways to handle those desires.

Parents and youth pastors need to get more inquisitive than directive when it comes to young people. Get curious. Ask questions. Teens are developing who they are, their identity, and sometimes adults get so caught up in feeling responsible to give right answers to questions young people aren't even asking. Instead, be more inquisitive about who they are becoming. Learn about them. Find out what *their* questions are.

Continued from page 51.

asked survey respondents to assess porn's impact on their relationships, not to report use or viewing of porn. Most sources, including previous Barna studies, agree that overall use is much more widespread than responses to this narrowly focused question might suggest. For example, 41% of practicing Christian men ages 13 to 24 report seeking out porn at least once a month.[8]) Those who have personally struggled with pornography or other sexual addictions are overwhelmingly more likely to report pornography as an issue in their relationships (43% vs. 3% of those with no experience). They are four times as likely (40% vs. 10%) to say addiction affects their most important relationships and at least twice as likely to say sexual intimacy (56% vs. 25%) and loneliness (57% vs. 28%) are relational issues for them.

This pattern is even more pronounced among practicing Christians. Every relational issue surfaces at a considerably higher rate among those with a spouse or child with pornography or other sexual addictions than among those who have personally experienced such struggles. This includes anxiety (84% vs. 55%), marriage problems (72% vs. 28%), depression (70% vs. 52%), sexual intimacy (69% vs. 41%), grief (66% vs. 37%), parenting problems (66% vs. 29%) and loneliness (62% vs. 50%).

Nearly half of those with direct experience of sexual addiction (49%) report that addiction affects their important relationships (vs. 5% among those with no experience). Those who have personal experience are also twice as likely as those with no experience to name anxiety (70% vs. 34%), depression (65% vs. 31%), loneliness (55% vs. 25%) and sexual intimacy (48% vs. 24%) as issues.

Cheating / Infidelity

Unsurprisingly, experiencing infidelity in a romantic relationship contributes to anxiety and / or depression. Those who have been cheated on are more likely than not to say anxiety (59% vs. 31% those without direct or indirect experience) and depression (57% vs. 27%), affect their relationships. Also more prevalent compared to those who have no experience of cheating are relational issues such as sexual intimacy (40% vs. 22%), grief (36% vs. 19%), marital problems (38% vs. 14%) and parenting problems (32% vs. 14%).

Divorce

Experiencing a divorce consistently shows the weakest correlation to increased relational issues. Although the correlation exists, it is notably smaller than other traumas investigated in the study. For some people, divorce may be a welcome solution to other types of trauma. But even when that's not the case, there is a rising trend of wanting to stay friends with one's ex.[9] In comparison to those with no experience of divorce, the increase in frequency of relational issues is significant. Among the general population, divorced people are more likely to experience problems with sexual intimacy (36% among ever divorced vs. 26% never divorced) and addiction (17% vs. 11%). For practicing Christians, the effects of divorce are more evident than in the general population in almost every area tested.

MORAL JUDGMENTS

So how do people morally assess their relational issues? Researchers asked participants about their current beliefs with regard to the morality of divorce and pornography, two issues with a history of moral freight in the Christian community. According to sociologist Samuel Perry, for example:

> Whereas many other Americans seem to be able to view porn without it causing significant mental health problems, for conservative Christians it's different. The church's zero-tolerance policy for porn means those who consume it only occasionally might see themselves as addicts from the first viewing. So even though

conservative Christians use porn less than other Americans, they are statistically twice as likely to consider themselves "addicted" to it. Their shame can be soul-crushing.[10]

The responses inside and outside the Church are similar, as the chart shows, with the general population leaning further toward the view that divorce is morally acceptable. Among practicing Christians, Millennials exhibit the most polarization; their generation is least inclined to give the middle response that divorce is "sometimes" permissible for Christians, and most likely to respond with the extremes "never" and "always."

The Morality of Divorce, U.S. Adults vs. Practicing Christians

○ ALWAYS   ○ OFTEN   ○ SOMETIMES   ○ SELDOM   ○ NEVER

Divorce can be permitted for a Christian.

U.S. adults

| 23% | 25% | 30% | 12% | 10% |

Divorce is morally acceptable.

Practicing Christians

| 17% | 19% | 35% | 16% | 14% |

n = 2,307 U.S. adults 18 and over, March–May 2019.

Our perceptions are inevitably shaped by life experience. Often, difficult situations can increase compassion and empathy and diminish moralistic judgment. Yet the human desire to preserve our opinion of ourselves can also lead us to downplay problems or give moral priority to the lens of our own experience. For those who have directly or indirectly experienced relational trauma such as divorce, infidelity, depression or anxiety, addiction, pornography or sexual addiction, a number of differences emerge compared with those who have no such experiences. For example, having been through a divorce correlates with one's attitude toward divorce. Those who have divorced are much more likely than those who have not been to view divorce as permissible. In the general population, there is a gap between the proportions of Gen X (38%) and Boomers (57%) who view divorce as morally acceptable, correlating with a spike in divorce rates commonly seen in these years.

The Morality of Divorce, Married vs. Divorced Adults

○ **ALWAYS**   ○ OFTEN   ○ SOMETIMES   ○ SELDOM   ○ **NEVER**

Divorce can be permitted for a Christian.

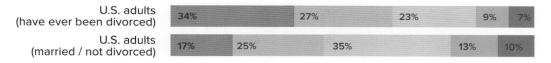

	ALWAYS	OFTEN	SOMETIMES	SELDOM	NEVER
U.S. adults (have ever been divorced)	34%	27%	23%	9%	7%
U.S. adults (married / not divorced)	17%	25%	35%	13%	10%

Divorce is morally acceptable.

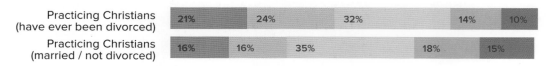

	ALWAYS	OFTEN	SOMETIMES	SELDOM	NEVER
Practicing Christians (have ever been divorced)	21%	24%	32%	14%	10%
Practicing Christians (married / not divorced)	16%	16%	35%	18%	15%

n = 2,307 U.S. adults 18 and over, March–May 2019.

   In contrast to the relative similarity inside and outside the Church with respect to divorce, practicing Christians' and the general population's views on the morality of pornography diverge sharply. Younger generations are more accepting of pornography use, but the majority of practicing Christian Millennials and Gen Z still says it is morally wrong.

Continued on page 64.

ANXIETY, DEPRESSION & AVOIDING PASTORAL BURNOUT

A Q&A with Rhett Smith

Q.

As someone with a background in both pastoral ministry and mental health, what do you think each uniquely brings to the table when it comes to restoring people and relationships to wholeness? What are some ways the two can work together more effectively?

A.

My mental health background equips me with the best tools and practices and my pastoral ministry background equips me with faith in the work of God in people's lives. I chose an American Psychological Association–approved seminary to do my theology and psychology work in order to get the best of both Christian and secular tools and practices, and to learn how to integrate my faith into the implementation and practice of them. The integration of these two—mental health / psychology and pastoral ministry / theology—provides me with two different lenses to view people's struggles in a more holistic way, and to help me frame healing and recovery from a holistic perspective.

I encourage those in pastoral ministry not to automatically judge secular mental health practices as unviable options for restoration, but instead use wisdom to find tools, practices and models of recovery that connect to their theology. I also encourage them not to simply hand over their expertise to those in the traditional healing practices (doctors, counselors, psychologists, and so on), but to value their training and expertise as giving them insights into the whole person that others may not have. And I encourage those in the mental health fields to realize that people's physical, emotional, mental and spiritual lives all need to be addressed in order for healing to happen—and pastoral ministry can provide rich wisdom in those areas.

Ultimately, I see mental health and pastoral ministry as perfect partners in the work of healing people and relationships. They see being human with different lenses—but when united, they reveal a fuller and clearer picture.

Q.

Researchers asked people what challenges impact their most important relationships. Across the board, anxiety and / or depression were the most frequently reported challenge. In your experience, what are the most common ways anxiety and / or depression impact relationships?

A.

Anxiety and depression are not feelings, but coping behaviors that a person resorts to when there are underlying violations around love (identity) and trust (safety).

So first, anxiety and depression impact relationships on a behavioral level. For example, sometimes people become perfectionistic in order to soothe their anxiety. Often that perfectionism has all kinds of impact on their relationships with others, creating conflict. Or if someone is depressed, they might withdraw and become emotionally flat and listless—and you can bet that has a huge impact on how someone relates to them.

Second, anxiety and depression impact relationships because the underlying core feelings that trigger those coping behaviors impact how a person sees themselves. For example, if someone feels not good enough or emotionally unsafe (two huge underlying feelings that can give rise to anxiety and depression), that feeling can become their identity. Being in relationship with someone who feels that way about themselves creates all kinds of relational issues.

Simply put, anxiety and depression impact relationships because they distort how we see ourselves and others. And that's a recipe for relational issues.

None of us are immune to anxiety and depression. If we haven't already, we will all experience the relational struggles these bring about at some point in our lives. The good news is that mental health and pastoral ministry can provide a beautiful model of healing for those who are suffering. The model I love and use is Restoration Therapy, and it has brought healing to tons of people.

Q.

In Barna's 2017 *The State of Pastors* study, we found that one in five U.S. Protestant pastors (21%) says they frequently feel mentally or emotionally exhausted, and about one in six (15%) rates their emotional health lower than excellent or good. What are some ways that pastors and other Christian leaders should care for their mental health?

A.

I typically encourage pastors and other Christian leaders to do three things. First, make sure to have a good practice of self-care for your physical, emotional, mental and spiritual life. It's important to sustain these four areas in a regular rhythm. For example, I might encourage a pastor to (physical) exercise three times a week, (emotional) have a date night with their spouse once a week, (mental) set aside time to read and learn and (spiritual) engage in a daily practice of prayer in solitude.

Second, I encourage them to see a therapist or spiritual director—someone who is trained to understand them holistically who can provide a confidential and safe place for them to be themselves. A place where they don't have to be the pastor or leader. This is essential. I'm surprised by the number of pastors who have

RHETT SMITH is a Licensed Marriage and Family Therapist and Certified Executive Coach in Plano, Texas. He is the author of *The Anxious Christian: Can God Use Your Anxiety for Good?* and works with churches and organizations to help improve their relationships, wellness and performance. Currently he is part of a collaborative effort to equip pastors and ministry leaders to help bring healing to those in their ministries suffering from anxiety and depression. He lives in Texas with his wife and two kids. You can check out his work at www.rhettsmith.com.

never done therapy or sat with a spiritual director. How can pastors and ministry leaders encourage others to seek out help if they haven't done it themselves, haven't experienced firsthand what it's like to be the helped instead of the helper?

Third, I encourage them to have an intimate community of trusted friends where they don't have to be pastor or ministry leader. Find a group of friends who ask tough questions and aren't "yes people." I wrote a paper in seminary about the moral failings of ministry leaders, and what I found in my research was that most hit their crisis point when they became isolated and exhausted.

If pastors and ministry leaders employ these three practices, they set themselves up for a more successful journey through the ups and downs of life and ministry.

Continued from page 59.

This is not the case outside the Church at all. According to Barna's study on views and use of porn, U.S. teens and young adults are more likely to say "not recycling" (56%) is immoral than to say so about "viewing pornographic images" (32%).[11]

Younger generations are more accepting of pornography use, but the majority of practicing Christian Millennials and Gen Z still says it is morally wrong

The Morality of Porn Use, U.S. Adults vs. Practicing Christians

◯ ALWAYS ◯ OFTEN ◯ SOMETIMES ◯ SELDOM ◯ NEVER

Pornography use is morally wrong.

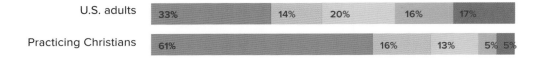

U.S. adults: 33% | 14% | 20% | 16% | 17%

Practicing Christians: 61% | 16% | 13% | 5% | 5%

n = 2,307 U.S. adults 18 and over, March–May 2019.

MENTAL HEALTH STRUGGLES & SOLUTIONS

As we've seen, mental health issues such as anxiety and depression can deeply affect relationships. Reciprocally, a relational issue such as infidelity can bear heavily on one's mental health, increasing anxiety and depression. Additionally, each person's worldview forms a lens through which these issues are perceived. More specifically, a Christian worldview seems to make a difference in how people think about mental health. In order to assess to what extent this is true, researchers presented a series of commonly held views and ideas about mental health and mental illness. (See graphs on pages 66-67.)

Practicing Christians express high confidence that, in a fallen world, anyone or everyone might face a relationship crisis. Their distribution of responses is similar to that of the general population, with slightly more saying it is "always true" that a relationship crisis could happen to anyone.

Practicing Christians, along with all U.S. adults, are supportive of the notion that physical, mental, sexual and spiritual health increase together. Christians, however, are more inclined to view them as interconnected, with more than half saying so (54% vs. 39%).

In line with such a view, practicing Christians also express higher degrees of openness to a range of possible helps for relational and mental difficulties. For example, they are more likely than the general population to say that counseling should be a part of any restoration or healing of relationship issues.

Practicing Christians are also slightly *more likely* to believe medication for anxiety or depression should always be taken, compared to the general population.

Only practicing Christians were asked about Bible reading and prayer as a solution to mental health problems, and their responses fall in a similar bell curve: "Sometimes" emerges as the most frequent response (42%) but, as with counseling and medication, attitudes lean toward the affirmative.

They also generally tend to agree that Christians should stick exclusively to things the Bible says or recommends when receiving counseling.

Practicing Christians' views on the spiritual aspect of mental well-being diverges from the views of the culture at large. Close to half of practicing Christians (47%) believe a closer walk with God is "always" or "often" the solution to mental health problems. Among the general population, respondents were asked to rate the degree to which they believe the solution to mental health problems is faith—and their responses tilt in the opposite direction. A plurality believes faith is "seldom" or "never" the solution (40%).

Since the earliest days of psychology, some Christians haven't been sure how to think about science-based mental health research and therapies. It has not always been clear how the findings and theories of psychology fit comfortably into a Christian worldview—and for a small minority of believers, that's still the case today. One in six practicing Christians would say evil spirits are often (10%) or always (8%) the cause of mental illness. Another one in four (27%) says this is sometimes the case. There is uncertainty here, which means there's room for pastors and trained counselors to help educate Christians about both mental illness and spiritual warfare.

Continued on page 71.

Perceptions About Mental & Emotional Health, U.S. Adults vs. Practicing Christians

○ ALWAYS ○ OFTEN ○ SOMETIMES ○ SELDOM ○ NEVER

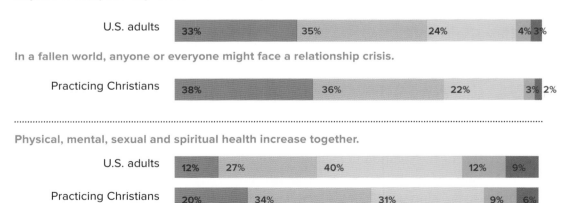

Anyone or everyone might face a relationship crisis.

U.S. adults — 33% | 35% | 24% | 4% | 3%

In a fallen world, anyone or everyone might face a relationship crisis.

Practicing Christians — 38% | 36% | 22% | 3% | 2%

Physical, mental, sexual and spiritual health increase together.

U.S. adults — 12% | 27% | 40% | 12% | 9%

Practicing Christians — 20% | 34% | 31% | 9% | 6%

Counseling should be a part of any restoration or healing of relationship issues.

U.S. adults
| 14% | 30% | 42% | 9% | 5% |

Practicing Christians
| 22% | 35% | 35% | 5% | 3% |

People should take medication for anxiety or depression.

U.S. adults
| 9% | 23% | 47% | 13% | 8% |

Christians should take medication for anxiety or depression.

Practicing Christians
| 12% | 23% | 46% | 11% | 8% |

The solution to mental health problems is Bible reading and prayer.

Practicing Christians
| 15% | 19% | 42% | 17% | 7% |

Christians should stick exclusively to things the Bible says or recommends when receiving counseling.

Practicing Christians
| 23% | 26% | 31% | 14% | 6% |

The solution to mental health problems is faith.

U.S. adults
| 9% | 13% | 38% | 20% | 20% |

The solution to mental health problems is a closer walk with God.

Practicing Christians
| 21% | 26% | 40% | 9% | 4% |

Mental health problems are caused by evil spirits.

Practicing Christians
| 8% | 10% | 27% | 21% | 34% |

n = 2,307 U.S. adults 18 and over, March–May 2019.

HEALING ADDICTION IN THE CHURCH

A Q&A with Tal Prince

Q.

There's ongoing debate around whether addiction is a disease or a choice. In your years of pastoring and then in counseling practice, which of these theories have you found comes closest to the mark?

A.

It's a disease of choice. The disease lives in the limbic system, which is also the brain's reward center. Its basic job is to keep you alive, but it does so based on 15-second time horizons. When the limbic system is making all of your decisions, it's the functional equivalent of a kindergarten classroom with no adult in the room. The frontal cortex is the adult—that's where executive command and control is—but it isn't fully working until your early 20s.

If you think of all addiction like a tree, there are a whole lot of branches on the outer tree. There are opiates, eating disorders, porn and so on. If I say, "Hey, you've got a drinking problem, you need to quit drinking," all I've said is that you should saw the alcohol branch off the tree.

But guess what? The branch is going to grow back. And while you wait, you're going to hang out on some other branches and develop some other addictions, because we're never addicted to just one thing. We're always multiply addicted.

To get rid of the addiction tree, we have to take it out at the roots. It's the root, not the branch, that is the real issue.

First, we dig the soil away. The soil is shame. No shame, no addiction; it's that simple. Then the roots are exposed. What we find at the root is abuse—verbal, mental, emotional, sexual or physical—and trauma. The tree of addiction can only be removed when we help people heal from those deep wounds.

Jesus is the best model of this approach. He says that if you give him your heart, he will change your behavior. But too often we want to make giving him our hearts *about* behavior modification. The gospel is not about behavioral modification.

Q.

There seems to be a disconnect between many pastors and mental health professionals. How do we work through and destigmatize the growing divide between these camps?

A.

We have to be very intentional about spending time dialoguing together, and that happens far too rarely. Our relationships with each other are not what they need to be. There's mistrust. But the poor state of intimacy in our culture demands that we work far more closely together.

Pastors can and should walk with people through all the tough stuff of being human and following Christ. But when the tough stuff is addiction, or cyclic repetition of family-of-origin abuse, or the aftermath of trauma or mental illness—a pastor needs support helping people deal with those kinds of issues. Clinical depression or anxiety requires more than trustworthy spiritual direction and discipleship practices, and pastors should partner with a mental health professional.

I think people tend to have a baseline assumption that their pastor should be able to help them when they're in crisis. They think, *he's super spiritual and knows the Bible, so he should be able to help us.*

Take addiction again, just because it's a great framework for thinking about these issues. Generally speaking, I think pastors and pastoral counselors are on solid ground when they are helping someone wrestle with curiosity and desire, but that they need to seek help from a mental health professional if and when habit becomes a part of the picture. Most pastors are not trained addiction counselors, domestic abuse social workers, trauma therapists or psychiatrists.

I'm part of a podcast in which we try to teach pastors when it's the time to refer congregants to outside professional help. Pastors need to know where the line is, but it's hard for them because the expectation is that they can fix it.

I've had pastor clients who are terrified they *can't* fix something, can't solve something, and are afraid to say they don't know. That's a terrible position for pastors to be in. If we can find a way for pastors and mental health pros to work together, they wouldn't find themselves in that position.

Both camps need to establish boundaries, respect each other and talk through issues together.

TAL PRINCE earned his masters of divinity from Beeson Divinity School and a masters in clinical mental health from the University of Alabama at Birmingham. He uses both degrees to preach and counsel regularly, and is in demand as a speaker on addictions, trauma and couples. He is director of Insights Counseling Center and lives with his wife and two daughters in Birmingham, Alabama.

Continued from page 66.

Generational Trends ━━━━━

Overall, practicing Christian Millennials are more open than older believers to a variety of ideas about and treatments for mental health problems. They are more likely to say that anyone could encounter a relationship crisis; that physical, mental, sexual and spiritual health increase together; that counseling should be a part of relational restoration and healing; and that both Bible reading and prayer and a closer walk with God are effective solutions.

In fact, agreement with these statements is more common among younger generations. Culturally speaking, this is not at all surprising. For many 20- and 30-somethings, emotional and mental health is on par with physical health: All are essential to a holistic sense of well-being. In Christian circles, as well, many writers and ministry practitioners of the past few decades have begun to connect spiritual growth with emotional and mental health, arguing that fruitful discipleship must entail growth in all these areas.

This is good news for anyone who is passionate about making young disciples. As young adults seek emotional well-being, Christians who can speak the language of mental and emotional health can help them connect to their spiritual lives, as well.

> As young adults seek emotional well-being, Christians who can speak the language of mental and emotional health can help them connect to their spiritual lives, as well

Stigma ━━━━━

It is one thing to acknowledge the benefits of counseling and another to actually seek out professional help. One barrier may be community stigma. Practicing Christians were asked whether they thought their pastor, priest and / or other people in their church community would want them to seek out professional counseling for a relationship crisis, and half of respondents (52%) feel a low degree of stigma, anticipating a high degree of support. A small minority (8%) feels a high degree of stigma, expecting that their church community would most likely not want them to pursue such assistance. There could be a range of underlying attitudes fueling such high stigma, such as "The problem isn't really a problem, so there is nothing to fix" and "The problem can be solved without a professional counselor."

A fair number (40%) falls in between, predicting some stigma if they were to seek professional help. This latter group, practicing Christians who perceive *some* degree of stigma toward seeking professional counseling, is the most likely among the three groups to respond "sometimes" when asked to evaluate each of the statements about mental and relational health. By contrast, the high stigma group is the most polarized, with a smaller percentage of respondents choosing the middle ground. They are not in lockstep agreement with each other, but they share strong feelings about these issues.

Practicing Christians with trauma experience are more likely to affirm that counseling should be a part of healing relationship issues

Personal Experience & Solutions ——————

Both inside and outside the Church, those with firsthand experience of trauma respond with stronger conviction that anyone may face a relationship crisis (39% vs. 28% "always true" practicing Christians with no experience; 36% vs. 18% all adults with no experience). Practicing Christians with trauma experience are also more likely than those without to affirm that physical, mental, sexual and spiritual health increase together (55% vs. 43%) and that counseling should be a part of healing relationship issues (59% vs. 45%).

When comparing those who have battled depression / anxiety with those who have not, the latter are more likely to feel that taking medication is *not* the solution. Both inside and outside the Church, one in nine (11%) feels that medication is "never" the solution, compared to one in 20 of those who have experienced depression / anxiety themselves (5%) and just three percent of those who have a loved one who has struggled in this area. Among practicing Christians, this trend strengthens in the "always" responses: Those who have indirectly experienced the effects of anxiety and depression via their loved ones are most likely to advocate medication (16%), compared to those who have no experience (11%).

Now that we know where people are feeling relational pressures, let's find out where they look for help.

3

WHERE DO PEOPLE TURN FOR SUPPORT & HOW CAN CHURCHES HELP?

Households of Faith, Barna's study on how people who share the same living space strengthen each other's spirituality, found that people who interact on a spiritual level—whether through prayer, Bible study or some other activity—are more likely than those who don't to turn toward one another during a personal crisis. In other words, there is at least "some correlation between sharing spiritual interactions and having each other's backs."[12]

Both inside and outside the Church, respondents to the *Restoring Relationships* survey say they are most likely to look to a family member or close friend (53%) for help with a relationship problem, whether the issue involves their spouse (56% all adults vs. 53% practicing Christians), their child (50% both), their parent (60% vs. 61%) or another loved one (61% vs. 62%).

Practicing Christians are more likely than U.S. adults overall to turn to a pastor or priest for relational support—and are also more likely to seek help from a professional counselor or therapist

Yet as the chart shows, practicing Christians are more likely than the national average to reach out to others for support. They are more likely to seek help from a professional counselor than are U.S. adults overall. They are also much more likely, as we would expect, to turn to their pastor or priest. On the other hand, adults from the general population are more likely to turn to internet resources for help.

Where Do You Turn for Help?, U.S. Adults vs. Practicing Christians
% among those who have experienced a relationship hardship

◯ U.S. ADULTS
◯ PRACTICING CHRISTIANS

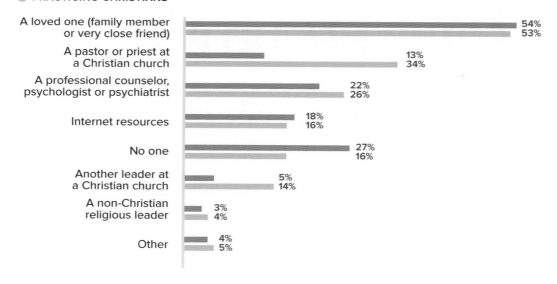

	U.S. ADULTS	PRACTICING CHRISTIANS
A loved one (family member or very close friend)	54%	53%
A pastor or priest at a Christian church	13%	34%
A professional counselor, psychologist or psychiatrist	22%	26%
Internet resources	18%	16%
No one	27%	16%
Another leader at a Christian church	5%	14%
A non-Christian religious leader	3%	4%
Other	4%	5%

n = 2,307 U.S. adults 18 and over, March–May 2019.

The lion's share hold optimistic expectations of church help. Three-quarters or more say leaders in their church "definitely" or "probably" truly care (86%), help people develop healthy relationships (76%), can be trusted with private or personal issues (78%), can be trusted to genuinely help with personal issues such as a relationship problem (76%) and are available to help with such issues (77%).

When researchers ask senior pastors who members of their congregation turn to for relationship help, church leaders tend to put themselves at the top of the list, rather than members' close friends. (This is probably less a case of thinking of themselves too highly than of not always knowing when they are being left out of the loop.)

Where Congregants Turn for Help, According to U.S. Pastors / Priests

○ ALWAYS ○ OFTEN ○ SOMETIMES

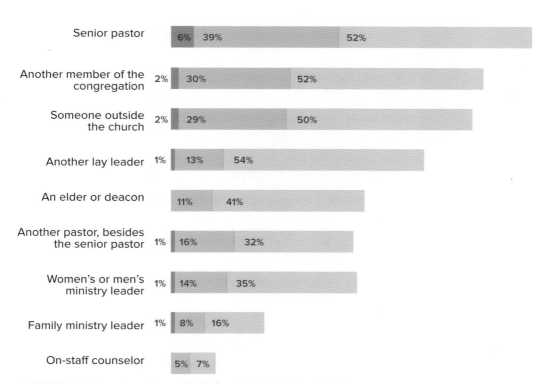

	ALWAYS	OFTEN	SOMETIMES
Senior pastor	6%	39%	52%
Another member of the congregation	2%	30%	52%
Someone outside the church	2%	29%	50%
Another lay leader	1%	13%	54%
An elder or deacon		11%	41%
Another pastor, besides the senior pastor	1%	16%	32%
Women's or men's ministry leader	1%	14%	35%
Family ministry leader	1%	8%	16%
On-staff counselor		5%	7%

n = 656 U.S. Protestant senior pastors and Catholic priests, March–April 2019.

When it comes to trust, pastors and priests have a fairly accurate sense of their parishioners' response: Three-quarters (74%) believe their congregants "definitely" or "probably" trust their church leaders to help them navigate a relationship challenge. As their tenure grows, so too does their perception of congregational trust. Although still a majority, fewer pastors (63%) who have shepherded their congregation for one to three years are confident of their congregants' trust compared to pastors with a tenure of four to nine years (74%). And those who have been with their congregation for a decade or more are most likely (81%) to say their congregants trust them.

Most pastors report counseling a significant number of parishioners, with more than one-third (36%) estimating that 10 percent or more of their congregation sought them out for relationship help in the past year, and more than one-quarter (28%) estimating five to 10 percent. Among pastors of fewer than 100 congregants, half say that 10 percent or more of their congregation requested pastoral support for their relationships (51%), compared to about one-third of mid-sized congregations (35%) and one in nine large-church leaders (11%). These percentages shake out to about the same level of counseling burden in absolute numerical terms, but small-church pastors are helping a larger proportion of their whole congregation.

WHAT KIND OF SUPPORT HELPS MOST

People turn to a range of sources for help with a relationship problem, and often seek help from more than one source. These sources can be grouped under three main headings: *professional* (a professional counselor, psychologist or psychiatrist), *spiritual* (a pastor, priest or other church leader) and *relational* (a family member or close friend). Grouping these kinds of support can help analysts better understand their overall effectiveness.

Turning to a spiritual source of support consistently correlates with more positive reports of satisfaction with relationships, of

Well-Being Among Those Who Have Sought Help
% "always" among practicing Christians

○ SOUGHT SPIRITUAL HELP ○ SOUGHT RELATIONAL HELP ○ SOUGHT PROFESSIONAL HELP

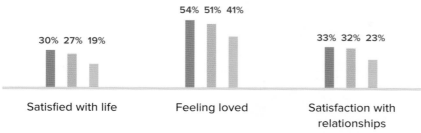

30% 27% 19% — 54% 51% 41% — 33% 32% 23%

Satisfied with life — Feeling loved — Satisfaction with relationships

n = 2,307 U.S. adults 18 and over, March–May 2019.

satisfaction with life and of feeling loved. (This section focuses mainly on practicing Christians, but these trends are also observed in the general population.) Satisfaction rates of those who turn only to professional help are lowest by comparison, with relational support falling between the other two types. A caveat: We want to caution against concluding that professional help is less effective. What does seem clear is that a holistic approach—one that accounts for the spiritual dynamics of relationships—is often more effective than one-dimensional help.

> Turning to a spiritual source of support consistently correlates with more positive reports of satisfaction in relationships, of satisfaction with life and of feeling loved

Many people turn to more than one type of help, and the same trend of satisfaction correlated to spiritual support holds in various combinations. Practicing Christians who turn to relational and spiritual (but not professional) help are most likely to "always" be satisfied with their relationships (36%), satisfied with life (30%) and feeling loved (61%). By contrast, those with relational and professional (but no spiritual) support are least likely to report "always" being satisfied

Continued on page 84.

EMOTIONAL HEALTH & SPIRITUAL FORMATION

A Q&A with Mike Boland

Q.

Does emotional health matter when it comes to the Christian life, to churches? Why should it be important to pastors and other ministry leaders to consider emotional health in people's lives?

A.

Tim Keller talks about the "sin under the sin." Loneliness is a prime example. It's is one of the top reasons people engage in unwanted sexual behavior. It's the "sin under the sin."

So much of sexual sin comes from a legitimate longing that gets distorted. If we just preach, "Men, stop looking at porn!" but don't look at those inner workings—if we don't see *why* people are struggling—we miss people and it becomes moralism.

The marketers in the porn industry are students of human desire. They know where people are struggling, and they're ready to exploit those struggles for profit.

We must also become students of human desire, in order to help people grow in godly maturity. As we preach the gospel, we could leave it at "follow Jesus" or we can try to go after the stuff underneath. The lens of emotional health shows us the desires, idols and struggles that are down below. And as we preach and lead into those deeper things, people gain a greater awareness of who they are and who God is.

I love the proactive nature of pastoring. As a counselor, someone comes in and you have to start where they are. But as a pastor, I'm already proactively pursuing the image of Christ in them; I don't have to wait for them to come up with something.

I'm living life with them. I'm instigating. I'm pursuing their maturity in every way. As a pastor, I feel like my job is more holistic. I'm not only thinking about that person and what has shaped them, but also how to steward the gospel in their lives.

I couldn't do that as effectively without paying attention to emotional health.

Q.

What part should emotional health play when it comes to leaders themselves?

A.

If a leader is emotionally unhealthy, the culture he or she creates is unhealthy. Emotionally healthy churches start with leaders. And that's why I think Jesus, in John 17, spends an entire chapter praying for his disciples, the ones who would continue his mission. He prays for them and for their health. That's his desire for the Church.

Pastors need to take our own stories seriously. One of our core values as a church is emotional health. As a leadership team, we know a lot about each other's struggles. We spend a lot of time together, talking about how we are doing.

What would it look like to make emotional health a normal thing to pursue, to make a part of your faith community?

There's a lot of pain caused by professionalism, the untouchableness of the pulpit. That stuff doesn't help in crisis, it doesn't help in the normal everyday hardships that people face. Let's take pastoring out of the professional world and bring it to reality, bring it into our everyday lives.

MIKE BOLAND is an assistant pastor at City Church Eastside in Atlanta, Georgia, and has trained in the Seattle School of Psychology and Theology. He grew up in a children's home before receiving a football scholarship from The Citadel in Charleston, South Carolina, and beginning a life in ministry. Mike, Jennifer and their four kids love their neighborhood and enjoy gathering with friends and neighbors around the dinner table. Mike enjoys playing most sports and journeying with people as they investigate their own stories and questions of faith.

WASHING THE WOUNDS OF RACIAL TRAUMA

A Q&A with Chris Williamson

Q.

Some churches are making intentional efforts to become more racially and ethnically diverse. Naturally, leaders in such congregations are more likely to counsel or provide pastoral care to people from a different cultural background than themselves. What is a healthy way for pastoral caregivers to consider race or ethnicity as a factor in mental health or relational issues? Or should it be considered at all?

A.

When someone says they're hurting, leaders need to validate that pain. Many people in leadership do not know what it's like to be a woman or a person of color, because they've never experienced it. To be fair, as an African American, I have not experienced what a white man goes through as he's trying to live the principles of Jesus. So I think it gets down to obeying Paul's instructions to bear one another's burdens. If one part of the Body is hurting, we all hurt.

If we're going to be pastoral caregivers, we have to believe that racial trauma is real. There are so many suffering from racial "battle fatigue." They come into church traumatized by what's happening in their neighborhood or at their job. They've gotten pulled over or followed by police. It's real. When they come to church, they're looking for people who will listen to and lament with them—not try to fix it.

A lot of us have been running around

trying to fix the problem, but I think we should consider Job's friends: They were cool until they started talking. They sat with him in his pain. Like Job, traumatized and hurting people in our churches don't need a sermon or a class. *Can't you just see that I'm hurting? Can you sit with me in this pain?*

DR. CHRIS WILLIAMSON is the founder and senior pastor of Strong Tower Bible Church, a multiracial fellowship in Nashville. He is author of two books, *Making Disciples Who Make a Difference* and *One But Not The Same: God's Diverse Kingdom Come Through Race, Class, and Gender*. Pastor Chris is a pioneer in "The Fuller Story" initiative in Franklin, Tennessee, to include the agonies and accomplishments of African Americans through historical markers in places of equal nobility around the city's Confederate monument. He and his wife, Dorena, live in Franklin and have four children.

John Burke talks about how when Paul was arrested in Philippi, the Roman jailer beat him and threw him and Silas jail (see Acts 16). Then God shook the prison, the doors flew open. And without being told, the jailer showed compassion and good sense enough to wash Paul's wounds—the wounds that he and the government he represented unjustly inflicted on the apostle.

When it comes to trauma from racism past and present, leaders need to be willing to wash the wounds. Whether you personally inflicted those wounds or they were perpetrated by the unjust system we're all a part of, they're there. And we are called to wash them.

Continued from page 79.

with their relationships (21%), being satisfied with life (13%) or feeling loved (23%).

Additionally, practicing Christians who turn to spiritual sources of support are less likely to distance themselves from a church during a personal crisis (71% "never"), compared to 57 percent of those with relational help and 43 percent with professional help.

This seems like a good time to remind us all that correlation does not imply causation. That is, seeking relationship support from a church leader doesn't necessarily *cause* greater relational satisfaction. What we can say, however, is that spiritual help plays an important role in subjective relationship satisfaction, a role that is sometimes overlooked by the wider culture.

Let's take a closer look at the kinds of help churches offer.

Pastoral Teaching & Counseling ————

How often are relationship topics raised at church? Four out of five practicing Christians say they received at least some teaching about marriage (86%) and parenting (81%). Seven in 10 say they heard teaching on addiction (70%), relationship crises (68%) and loneliness (67%) at church, followed by three out of five who heard about anxiety (63%) or depression (62%). Significantly fewer recall hearing about singleness (53%), pornography (47%) or sexual intimacy (42%); more than half say they have "never" heard church leaders talk about pornography (53%) or sexual intimacy (58%). This is a missed opportunity to speak into people's lives about issues that impact their everyday realities and relationships.

Six in 10 practicing Christians whose church leaders talked about sensitive topics say that those conversations were helpful (60%). About one-quarter (23%) says it was neither helpful nor harmful, and 16 percent say the church's discussions were a mixed bag—sometimes helpful, sometimes harmful. If more pastors can learn biblically and relationally sound ways to talk about tough topics, this represents a real opportunity to engage more with struggling churchgoers.

Congregants' reports align fairly well with what pastors say. Of the topics included in the survey, marriage and parenting are most often covered in their teaching. Eighty-six percent of pastors address marriage at least once a year, including 55 percent who did so more than twice a year. Eighty-one percent address parenting at least annually, and 50 percent more than twice annually. Pornography, healthy sexuality and singleness, topics pastors address less frequently, are also the issues congregants report hearing about least. Singleness is least likely to be addressed by a pastor (41% at least once a year, including

How Often Do You Teach on Each Topic?, U.S. Pastors / Priests

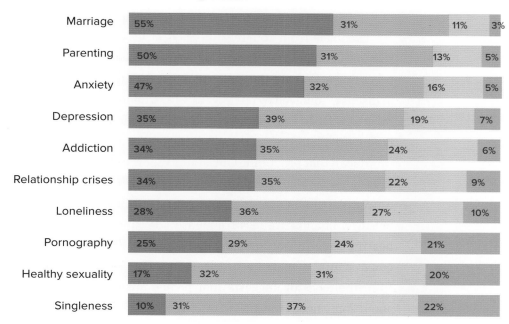

- MORE THAN TWICE A YEAR
- ONCE OR TWICE A YEAR
- LESS THAN ONCE A YEAR
- NEVER

Topic	More than twice a year	Once or twice a year	Less than once a year	Never
Marriage	55%	31%	11%	3%
Parenting	50%	31%	13%	5%
Anxiety	47%	32%	16%	5%
Depression	35%	39%	19%	7%
Addiction	34%	35%	24%	6%
Relationship crises	34%	35%	22%	9%
Loneliness	28%	36%	27%	10%
Pornography	25%	29%	24%	21%
Healthy sexuality	17%	32%	31%	20%
Singleness	10%	31%	37%	22%

n = 656 U.S. Protestant senior pastors and Catholic priests, March–April 2019.

10% more than twice a year) and most likely to be omitted altogether (22% never). (Many single Christians attest to this omission.) Again, this gap represents room for churches to stretch into areas where people would like gospel-centered help for their everyday lives.

Pastors' choice of topics is linked to their awareness of congregational needs. Pastors who discuss sensitive topics frequently with their church also more often report believing their congregants struggle with those sorts of things. For example, those who talk about marriage, singleness, parenting and healthy sexuality at least once a year are more likely to perceive marriage problems (62% vs. 43% pastors who address marriage less often), parenting problems (65% vs. 42%), issues with sexual intimacy (30% vs. 17%) or unwanted singleness (24% vs 19%) among their congregants. Pastors who teach on anxiety and depression at least once a year have a greater tendency than those who seldom or never address these issues to see anxiety (62% vs. 39%) or depression (53% vs. 29%) as common problems.

Feedback from congregants plays at least some role in shaping a pastor's perception of their congregation's needs. Marriage (70%) and parenting (67%) are the topics most pastors report being "encouraged to discuss," followed by anxiety (61%) and depression (56%). Pastors are most likely to be "discouraged to discuss"—whether directly or indirectly—topics related to healthy sexuality (5%) and pornography (6%).

Recall that practicing Christians report anxiety and depression as the top issues that impact their relationships, followed by loneliness, unwanted singleness, grief and sexual intimacy. Marriage and parenting problems are less frequently identified as causing problems, beating out only pornography and addiction. This mismatch between congregants' personal struggles and what they'd like to hear about from their pastor suggests that people are willing to be vulnerable about some needs more than others.

Also a factor is a pastor's sense of adequacy and preparedness to help people with certain issues. Barna's *The State of Pastors* study found that "counseling / people problems" is the top area of ministry for which pastors wish they had been better prepared.[13] Except for a death in the family, a majority in the *Restoring Relationships* pastor cohort says they feel only "somewhat equipped" to help someone navigate their relational difficulty. One in five reports feeling "not at all equipped" to handle unwanted prolonged singleness (21%), issues with sexual intimacy (21%) and addiction (19%). When it comes to churchgoers' struggles with anxiety and depression, two-thirds of pastors say they feel "somewhat equipped" to help. There is a correlation between feeling equipped to navigate depression or anxiety and talking more frequently about mental health. One-quarter of those who talk about mental illness at least once a year (25%) feels "very equipped," while just one in 10 of those who seldom talk about depression or anxiety (10%) feels the same confidence.

Pastors who feel equipped to talk about mental health teach about it at least once a year, but those who don't feel confident teach about it less frequently

Overall, non-mainline pastors feel more equipped to guide people through relationship difficulties than mainline leaders. This is a particular area of strength for evangelical and charismatic pastors, whose theological traditions emphasize the personally transformational aspects of the gospel—and whose witness is worth celebrating!

And here's some additional encouragement for church leaders: Among practicing Christians who have sought out a church leader for help with a relationship problem, a large majority (83%) says he or she handled the knowledge of their trouble "well" or "very well."

Given that pastors and priests are typically seen as responsible for pastoral care, it is encouraging and appropriate that the overwhelming majority (94%) has received some kind of training in this area. Formal coursework is the most common means, with almost two-thirds (64%) having received class training; most pastors with seminary degrees say counseling coursework was part of their degree program (70%), indicating that seminaries recognize the need to equip their graduates to

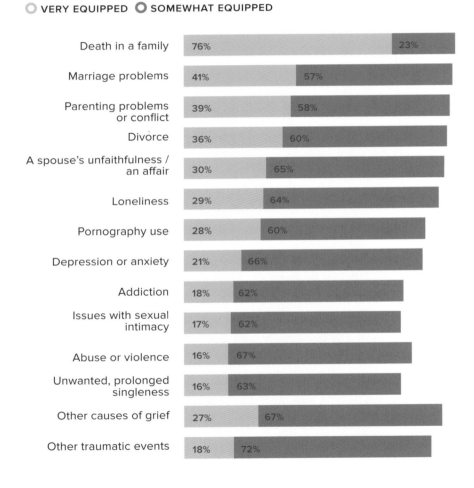

How Well Equipped Are You to Address Each Topic?, U.S. Pastors / Priests

○ VERY EQUIPPED ○ SOMEWHAT EQUIPPED

Topic	Very Equipped	Somewhat Equipped
Death in a family	76%	23%
Marriage problems	41%	57%
Parenting problems or conflict	39%	58%
Divorce	36%	60%
A spouse's unfaithfulness / an affair	30%	65%
Loneliness	29%	64%
Pornography use	28%	60%
Depression or anxiety	21%	66%
Addiction	18%	62%
Issues with sexual intimacy	17%	62%
Abuse or violence	16%	67%
Unwanted, prolonged singleness	16%	63%
Other causes of grief	27%	67%
Other traumatic events	18%	72%

n = 656 U.S. Protestant senior pastors and Catholic priests, March–April 2019.

serve in this area. Slightly more than half of senior pastors and priests (55%) have received on-the-job training in therapy, counseling or congregational care. A small minority has completed supervised clinical work (11%), earned a master's degree in therapy or counseling (6%) or obtained a therapist license (1%).

Most senior pastors say they and other ministry leaders participated in some kind of training for relationship counseling at least once in the past three years. Books and media about fostering healthy relationships and / or mental health are by far the most common resource: Three-quarters of senior pastors and priests (78%) and one-third of other church leaders (35%) have turned to a book or other media for training. Half of senior pastors and (49%) one-quarter of other leaders (27%) attended a conference within the past three years. Local training through one's church is utilized by 43 percent of pastors and one-quarter of other leaders (24%).

> When churches offer some kind of in-house counseling services, practicing Christians show greater confidence in the trustworthiness of their church as a source of relational support

IN-HOUSE COUNSELING & REFERRALS

Pastors whose churches offer in-house counseling—whether pastoral or professional—are more likely to say they feel "very equipped" to help their congregants navigate each of the relational issues (an increase of eight to 20 percentage points, compared to churches without in-house counseling). Seventy-one percent of senior pastors say they offer pastoral counseling themselves; one in five says another pastor on staff offers pastoral counseling (19%); and one in 10 says a professional counselor is available at the church. Two-thirds say they refer to professionals outside the church (64%). A small minority (6%) says they offer no counseling services at all.

Continued on page 93.

HEALTHY WAYS TO HELP THE OPPOSITE SEX

A Q&A with Thema S. Bryant-Davis and Cameron Lee

Q.

Nearly nine out of 10 Protestant pastors are men. At the same time, women are more likely than men to reach out to a pastor for relational help (many men say they prefer to read a book or search online for help). Do you think the gender disparity matters? In what ways has the imbalance has been detrimental or beneficial?

A.

BRYANT-DAVIS: The gender disparity matters because too often men lack awareness, sensitivity, compassion and training on issues that are more likely to face women: sexual harassment, sexism, depression, anxiety, PTSD, sexual abuse, intimate partner abuse, body image, infertility, miscarriage, sexual assault and workplace discrimination. This is detrimental when women congregants experience victim blaming, a lack of adequate concern for their safety and distress, and bad theology that can take the form of spiritual abuse. There are no benefits to only having male religious leaders available.

LEE: The disparity matters. From the help-giving side, the imbalance can create unrecognized norms of pastoral care. For example, does the pastor emphasize toughening up one's faith or building a relationship of empathy? It's not strictly either / or, of course, but the direction the pastor leans can affect his or her ability to connect with the person seeking help.

From the other side, there are also gendered norms in help-seeking. A man may say that he prefers to get help from a book or website. But that's not just a purely individual preference; it's a response to perceived norms (men aren't supposed to *need* help). Many men would welcome a more personal form of help—but only in a context in which it is safe to be vulnerable.

Both male and female pastors are capable of developing the skills and perspectives needed to connect with a wide range of people. But the existing disparity among pastors can tilt help-giving norms in a stereotypically male direction. The result is missed opportunities to establish better relational connections, or even to shift a congregation's culture toward greater emotional safety.

Q.

What do you wish pastors knew about mental illness and treatment? What is the one thing they could do more or less of to help churchgoers flourish in this area?

A.

BRYANT-DAVIS: Pastors should know that mental illness is not an indicator of lack of faith. People can have great faith and love for God and still live with depression, bipolar disorder, anxiety or schizophrenia. Therapy is not counter to the Christian faith, and ministers should not dissuade people from getting help. Therapy, prayer and reading the Bible can work together and are not at odds with one another. Just as studying the scriptures does not tell you everything you need to know about dentistry, plumbing and engineering, study of scripture alone does not give you all the information needed to address psychiatric disorders.

It is important for churches to be comfortable making referrals to mental health agencies to complement the services of pastoral care that are offered through the church. Churches could invite mental health professionals to provide workshops at the church. They could include information about mental health in bulletins, announcements, prayers and sermons.

Church leaders, including pastors, can seek mental health services themselves—many are facing great stress with limited support. They can commit to not preaching sermons that joke about or dismiss mental health concerns.

LEE: The first and most important step would be to reduce the inherent social stigma that is attached to mental illness so that sufferers don't feel they have to hide or pretend in order to be accepted and loved. Mental illness wears many guises and is much more common than we like to admit. A recent government report estimated that in 2018 roughly one out of every five adults in the United States suffered from some form of mental illness.[14]

Imagine, then, a congregation of 100 people; 20 of them may be suffering clinical levels of anxiety or depression or less common disorders like schizophrenia. They are part of the worshiping and serving community, but is it safe for them to admit their struggles? If they did, would they be shunned or avoided? Would they be told that they weren't being faithful enough, weren't praying enough or that they were demon-possessed?

These are all responses that the mentally ill have endured in their churches—responses that often discourage them from pursuing the treatment they need. Pastors can help by examining the explicit and implicit theology of their own congregations and asking themselves what they might do to increase awareness and compassion and reduce stigma and isolation.

THEMA S. BRYANT-DAVIS, PhD, is professor of psychology at Pepperdine University and is an ordained elder in the African Methodist Episcopal Church.

CAMERON LEE, PhD, is professor of family studies at Fuller Theological Seminary, where he has taught since 1986. He is author of nine books, including three on the life of pastors and their families, and serves as a teaching pastor himself. As a Certified Family Life Educator, he regularly conducts marriage and relationship workshops in congregations.

Continued from page 89.

When churches offer some kind of in-house counseling services, practicing Christians show greater confidence in the trustworthiness of their church as a source of support. These congregants are more likely to say their church can "definitely" be trusted with private or personal issues than those whose church offers no counseling services (60% vs. 27%). They are also more likely to say their church can be trusted to help with such issues (57% vs. 49%), that their church "definitely" cares about people (70% vs. 59%) and helps people develop healthy relationships (51% vs. 39%), and that their church is available to help with personal issues like a relationship problem (57% vs. 50%). They are also more likely to say it's helpful when church leaders address sensitive topics related to relationship problems and to credit their church with strengthening their faith "a lot."

Unsurprisingly, practicing Christians who have a personal relationship with their pastor are more likely than those who don't to also respond positively in these areas. Both in-house counseling and a personal connection with a pastor bolster the reputation of the church as a safe haven.

Drawing Close to or Backing Away from Church

More often than not, practicing Christians' relationship with their church deepens during relational difficulty. Among those who remember their relationship with the church moving in one direction or another, seven in 10 say they have grown closer to a church because of a personal crisis (69% vs. 31% who have not). This positive indication of effective support, however, is tempered by also noting that one-third recalls having distanced themselves from a church during a personal crisis (33% vs. 67% who have not).

Pastors are aware of both outcomes. Almost all pastors know of someone who has gotten closer to the church they shepherd because of a personal crisis (95% vs. 5% who say they do not know of someone for whom this is true). On the other hand, more than eight in 10 can recall someone who has distanced themselves from the church they lead as the result of a personal crisis (83% vs. 17% who say they do not know of someone for whom this is true).

Sadly, the top reason given by practicing Christians who have distanced themselves from a church is "I felt I couldn't be honest about myself and my life" (35%). Other reasons center on relational discord, including disagreement with church teaching (17%), disliking treatment by church leaders (15%) and disliking treatment by other congregants (16%).

A closer look at those who have distanced themselves during a personal crisis—a group that tends to trend lower in age—reveals a population with numerous relational challenges. They acknowledge having difficult childhoods that negatively impact their present-day relationships (32% vs. 14% those who have not distanced themselves from church). They are less likely to have always felt loved (49% vs. 63%), safe (47% vs. 65%) and understood (17% vs. 29%) while they were growing up, and more likely to have felt lonely (28% vs. 12%). At present they are also less likely to presently feel loved always (44% vs. 58%), satisfied with their relationships (70% vs. 81%) and satisfied with life (65% vs. 82%). They are more likely to have been touched by trauma related to divorce (43% vs. 38%), infidelity (56% vs. 28%), depression or anxiety (73% vs. 43%), addiction (42% vs. 19%) and pornography or sexual addiction (28% vs. 15%).

Good leadership means leading by example. The more pastors honestly talk about the real stuff of relationships, the more people will know that honest talk is how it's supposed to be done.

Hearteningly, separating from a particular church does not necessarily mean people give up on church altogether. One in five says they looked for another church after leaving the one where they didn't find the support they were seeking (20%).

In many cases, pastors can have enormous influence on church-goers' relationship to the church during relational crises. Consider this: If a church leader is honest and forthcoming about his or her own struggles, "I felt I couldn't be honest about myself and my life" is less likely to be an inhibiting issue for congregants! So often, good leadership means leading by example—and that includes healthy, godly ways of dealing with problems. The more pastors honestly talk about the real stuff of relationships, the more people will know that honest talk is the way forward.

CONCLUSION

PARTNERS IN RESTORATION

Churches are locally situated and supernaturally equipped to meet people's relational needs—and encouraging data from practicing Christians suggest many churches are already doing so. And, as we've seen, Christians aren't the only people who turn to churches for help. More than half of pastors (54%) say between one and five people who are not regular attenders sought their help with a relationship problem in the past year. One-quarter (24%) reports six or more non-church people asked for their help.

Counseling is an area where churches can increase their relational reach and service to their community, particularly because anxiety and depression are such widespread issues inside and outside the Church. But most small- and medium-size churches can't afford a full-time staff person dedicated to pastoral counseling. Here are some ideas for meeting relational and mental health needs in your community:

- **Find a partner.** Counseling is emotionally, mentally and spiritually demanding work, and sharing the load is a good idea. Is there a mental health professional already in your congregation? Or a state-licensed Christian counseling center in your community? Start a relationship so that you can make referrals to someone you trust. Know the limits of your expertise and lean on trusted others whose expertise complements your own.

- **Use all your resources.** Speaking of people in your church, what do they have to offer? It's a safe bet that at least one or two are in recovery from addiction of some kind, and 100-percent guaranteed that the long- and happily married have navigated some serious relationship problems. How can you connect them with people who are struggling now?
- **Connect groups.** In the same vein, people who are in touch with others on a regular basis report greater emotional and relational well-being, so make sure there are high-touch opportunities beyond Sunday morning. This is especially important for single people, who often need married folks and families to make special efforts to enfold them into the regular goings-on of life.
- **Train.** You may have had a pastoral counseling class in seminary, but there is so much more to learn! Whether it's through Pepperdine's Boone Center for the Family or another trustworthy source, deepen your knowledge, acquire new skills and get connected with other pastors and counselors who can help you live more deeply into your calling to shepherd people well.
- **Focus on anxiety and depression.** At least one-third of your faith community is dealing with one or the other—or both—and it's making a profound impact on their relationships. Get informed about these very common problems. Start talking about mental health from the pulpit. Encourage people under your pastoral care to get clinical help when they need it.
- **Talk about the hard stuff.** When Christians have heard their pastor teach on relational issues, they are more likely to say their church has helped them through relational crisis. Your words make a difference! So, go ahead and talk about sensitive topics, even if it makes people (including you) uncomfortable. Be discerning about when it might be helpful to talk about your own

struggles. People will be more likely to talk about the tough stuff in their own lives and ask for help when the tough stuff is too much.

- **Get the word out.** A significant percentage of churchgoers says they don't know what counseling options their own church has to offer. Let them know—so that when (not if) problems arise, they know already that they are not alone.

This study's findings strongly suggest that churches help people live better relational lives. In fact, people who seek out spiritual help for their relational problems report the best outcomes. Pastor, keep up the good work.

But the data also show that professional counseling and mental healthcare also play a vital role in helping people heal from trauma, addiction, mental illness and other deep hurts. God is using all of the above to restore broken people and broken relationships. That's good news!

Let's employ an all-of-the-above policy when it comes to restoring relationships—and rejoice to see the gospel come alive in everyday life!

>○○○<

A. NOTES

1.   Robert Putnam, *Bowling Alone: The Collapse and Revival of American Community* (New York: Simon & Schuster, 2000).

2.   "New Cigna Study Reveals Loneliness at Epidemic Levels in America," Cigna, https://www.cigna.com/newsroom/news-releases/2018/new-cigna-study-reveals-loneliness-at-epidemic-levels-in-america (accessed Nov. 2019).

3.   Barna Group, *The Connected Generation* (Ventura, CA: Barna Group, 2019).

4.   Timothy Keller, *The Meaning of Marriage* (New York: Penguin Books, 2011), 197.

5.   Keller, *The Meaning of Marriage*, 11.

6.   Paige Benton, "Singled Out by God for Good," *PCPC Witness* (February 1998) https://static.pcpc.org/articles/singles/singledout.pdf (accessed Nov. 2019).

7.   Quoted in Johann Hari, *Lost Connections: Why You're Depressed and How to Find Hope* (New York: Bloomsbury, 2018).

8.   Barna Group, *The Porn Phenomenon* (Ventura, CA: Barna, 2016).

9.   Ashley Fetters, "The Evolution of the Desire to Stay Friends with Your Ex," *The Atlantic*, August 19, 2019, https://www.theatlantic.com/family/archive/2019/08/why-do-people-want-stay-friends-after-breakup/596170/ (accessed Nov. 2019).

10. Janna Riess, "Conservative Christians Have a Porn Problem, Studies Show, But Not the One You Think," *Religion News Service*, August, 6, 2019, https://religionnews.com/2019/08/06/conservative-christians-have-a-porn-problem-studies-show/ (accessed Sept. 2019).

11. Barna Group, *The Porn Phenomenon*.

12. Barna Group, *Households of Faith* (Ventura, CA: Barna Group, 2019), 90.

13. Barna Group, *The State of Pastors*, (Ventura, CA: Barna Group, 2017), 66.

14. "Mental Health by the Numbers," the National Alliance on Mental Illness, September 2019. https://www.nami.org/learn-more/mental health-by-the-numbers (accessed Nov. 2019).

B. METHODOLOGY

U.S. ADULTS

Practicing Christians are self-identified Christians who say their faith is very important in their lives and have attended a worship service within the past month.

Generations

Gen Z were born after 1999.

Millennials were born between 1984 and 1999.

Gen X were born between 1965 and 1983.

Boomers were born between 1946 and 1964.

Elders were born in 1945 or earlier.

Parents include those who say they have children, regardless of child's age.

PASTORS

Mainline churches include American Baptist Churches, Episcopal, Evangelical Lutheran Church of America, United Church of Christ, United Methodist and Presbyterian Church, U.S.

Non-mainline churches include Protestant churches not included in mainline.

Small church: Less than 100 adults attend weekend services

Mid-sized church: Between 100 and 249 adult attenders

Large church: Churches with more than 250 attenders

METHODOLOGY

The research from this study includes a total of 2,307 online interviews with U.S. adults ages 18 and older, including 1,003 interviews with all adults in the general population and an additional 1,304 interviews with practicing Christians. Combined with the number of adults who qualified among the general population (n=219), the total number of interviews among practicing Christians is 1,523.

In order to qualify as a practicing Christian, respondents had to identify as Christian, agree strongly that their faith is very important in their life today and report attending a Christian church service at least once in the past month. The margin of error among the general population sample (n=1,003) is ±2.9 percentage points at the 95-percent confidence level. The margin of error among the practicing Christian sample (n=1,523) is ±2.3 percentage points at the 95-percent confidence level.

Interviews were conducted between March 27 to May 3, 2019. Respondents were invited from a randomly selected group of people matching the demographics of the U.S. population for maximum representation. Researchers set quotas to obtain a minimum readable sample by a variety of demographic factors and then minimally weighted the data by ethnicity, education and gender to reflect their natural presence in the known population, using U.S. Census Bureau data for comparison.

The research also includes 656 interviews among U.S. clergy, including 604 interviews with Protestant senior pastors and 52 with Catholic priests. Interviews were conducted between March 19 and April 26, 2019. These pastors were recruited from Barna's pastor panel (a database of pastors recruited via probability sampling on annual phone and email surveys) and are representative of U.S. Protestant and Catholic churches by region, denomination and church size. The margin of error among pastors is ±3.7 percentage points at the 95-percent confidence level.

ACKNOWLEDGMENTS

The Barna team sincerely thanks Sharon Hargrave, Kelly Haer, Elijah Weaver and the whole team at the Boone Center for the Family at Pepperdine University. Your passion for this research and how it will serve the Church has been an inspiration throughout the project. We also wish to thank our generous contributors, without whose expertise and insights this report would be considerably less practical: Katelyn Beaty, Michael Boland, Thema Bryant-Davis, Michael Cox, Cameron Lee, Tal Prince, Rhett Smith and Chris Williamson.

The Boone Center team extends heartfelt thanks to the following partners, whose generosity made this project possible: Pat Boone, Joline and Jim Gash, Debby and Andy Benton, Paula and Ed Biggers, Sheila and Tom Bost, Rita and Dale Brown, Lauren Cosentino, Susan Giboney, Geannie Holden-Sheller, Sara and Sam Jackson, Loretta and Robert Katch, Chris and Charlie Kerns, Leslie and John McKee, Marnie Mitze, Kimberly and Michael Okabayashi, Gary Oliver, Annette Oltmans, Claudia Preston, Joyce and Cliff Penner, Mary Alice Reed, Jenny and Fred Ricker, Jennifer and Rich Sittel, Scott Stanley, Carol and Robert Wallace, and Norm Wright.

The research team for *Restoring Relationships* is Brooke Hempell, Savannah Kimberlin, David Kinnaman and Pam Jacob. Under the editorial direction of Alyce Youngblood, Aly Hawkins and Joan Chen-Main wrote the report, and Doug Brown served as proofreader. Traci Hochmuth and Aly Hawkins created the data visualizations, which were designed, along with the full report, by Annette Allen. OX Creative designed the cover. Mallory Holt managed the project while Brenda Usery managed production. The *Restoring Relationships* team thanks our Barna colleagues Amy Brands, Daniel Copeland, Aidan Dunn, Janet Eason, Kristin Jackson, Joe Jensen, Steve McBeth, Rhesa Storms, Verónica Thames, Jess Villa and Todd White.

ABOUT THE PROJECT PARTNERS

Barna Group is a research firm dedicated to providing actionable insights on faith and culture, with a particular focus on the Christian church. In its 35-year history, Barna has conducted more than one million interviews in the course of hundreds of studies, and has become a go-to source for organizations that want to better understand a complex and changing world from a faith perspective.

Barna's clients and partners include a broad range of academic institutions, churches, nonprofits and businesses, such as Alpha, the Templeton Foundation, Fuller Seminary, the Bill and Melinda Gates Foundation, Maclellan Foundation, DreamWorks Animation, Focus Features, Habitat for Humanity, The Navigators, NBC-Universal, the ONE Campaign, Paramount Pictures, the Salvation Army, Walden Media, Sony and World Vision. The firm's studies are frequently quoted by major media outlets such as *The Economist,* BBC, CNN, *USA Today,* the *Wall Street Journal,* Fox News, Huffington Post, *The New York Times* and the *Los Angeles Times.*

Barna.com

The Boone Center for the Family is a training and resource center dedicated to restoring healthy relationships. Located in the heart of Malibu at Pepperdine University, the Boone Center for the Family integrates psychological research and theological principles to address today's relational needs. The center has programs for leaders of churches, Christian organizations and academic institutions through which they offer onsite trainings, webinars and published resources. In a world replete with relational roadblocks, disconnection, and trauma, the center firmly believes that the integration of psychology and theology provides a powerful pathway to restore healthy human connections.

The programs are designed to educate, equip and empower leaders to develop and teach healthy relationship skills. The RelateStrong program helps leaders understand their own relationship dynamics, while providing them with tools to help their communities strengthen relationships with spouses, family members, friends and colleagues. The RelateStrong | Leadership Series features a summit and supporting content designed to help church leaders discuss the growing and often difficult topics of addiction, parenting, marriage, pornography, sexual intimacy, singleness, depression and anxiety.

BooneCenter.Pepperdine.edu

BarnaAccess

For you to stay relevant, you have to be informed.

We're excited to announce a new, more affordable way for you to stay current on the best of what Barna is uncovering. It's called Barna Access.

Access is the most innovative way for you to stay informed. It's an exclusive collection of our growing library of research and also includes practical leadership resources.

With Access, you'll get:

- All of our best-selling monographs and new reports as they release
- Presentation slide decks that walk through key findings from each report
- Downloadable supporting resources including hundreds of infographics, expert commentaries, video interviews, white papers and articles

Subscribe at access.barna.com

Faith for the Future Church Kit

Ignite a movement of flourishing, resilient Christianity

With this kit, you can:

- Minister effectively to an anxious generation
- Raise up the next generation of leaders
- Equip young adults to follow Christ in the digital age

This kit combines insights from two innovative Barna studies: *The Connected Generation* and *Faith for Exiles*. It has everything you need to turn these world class insights into action with your leadership team or congregation.

The package contains: *The Connected Generation* global report (1 print copy and 5 digital licenses), all Country / Region Reports, presenter slides from the Faith for the Future webcast event, downloadable field guides for group discussion and personal reflection and free access to two Barna ecourses: *Making Resilient Disciples for Churches* and *Raising Resilient Disciples for Parents*. This is $370 in resources for one low price!

**Purchase at
theconnectedgeneration.com**